Guiding Your Child Toward God

Guiding Your Child Toward God

C. Sybil Waldrop

BROADMAN PRESS
Nashville, Tennessee

Dewey Decimal Classification: 649
Subject Headings: CHILD DEVELOPMENT // CHILDREN—RELIGIOUS
LIFE
Library of Congress Card Catalog Number: 84-14964
Printed in the United States of America

Library of Congress Cataloging in Publication Data

Waldrop, C. Sybil.
    Guiding your child toward God.

    1. Christian education of children. I. Title.
BV1475.2.W35   1985   248.8′4   84-14964
ISBN 0-8054-5660-0 (pbk.)

This book is affectionately dedicated to my family

- my beloved parents, Annie B. Sanders and B. Paul Durbin, who from birth lovingly guided me toward God
- my faithful husband, Fred Donald, who encouraged with words and actions my freedom to become fully the person God made me able to become
- my loving children, Don, LeAnn, and Mark, whom I have had the privilege of guiding toward God
- my adorable grandchildren, McIntyre and Heather, who have blessed my life with love
- and to my devoted friend, tireless teacher, and co-laborer Alma May Scarborough, who is a radiant example of Christian joy

Contents

We are partners working together for God (1 Cor. 3:9).

A Personal Word

Welcome to the joys of parenthood! You have just embarked on life's most challenging and rewarding experience—training up your child in the way he should go. "Train up a child in the way he should go: and when he is old, he will not depart from it" (Prov. 22:6). What does "in the way he should go" mean in this verse? *The Amplified Bible* uses the words "[and in keeping with his individual gift or bent]." The Keil-Delitzsch translation from the original language says, "Give to the child instruction conformably to His way; So he will not, when he becomes old, depart from it."

As a parent, you may have a greater influence on your child than any other person in the world. "Children are a gift from the Lord" (Ps. 127:3, GNB)—a real blessing. God has granted you one of His choicest blessings.

God makes parents responsible and accountable for each gift He gives. You become your child's first teacher. You are responsible to protect, nurse, comfort, guide, instruct, encourage, and meet his needs with tender loving care.

Your newborn depends on you for nourishment to sustain her physical growth. She depends on you for warmth and comfort to help her feel secure in her new surroundings. She depends on you to handle her gently, play with her joyfully, talk to her softly and playfully, and look happily into her eyes to stimulate her thinking and help her feel loved.

The way a newborn relates to his earthly parents illustrates in earthly form the way in which you, the parent, relate to God, your Heavenly Father. As your child is totally dependent upon you for his life, you are totally dependent upon God, your Heavenly Father, for your life. May your love be like God's—patient, kind, giving, caring, forgiving, and loving! "The Lord is not slack concerning his promise, as some men count slackness; but is longsuffering to us-ward, not willing that any should perish, but that all should come to repentance" (2 Pet. 3:9).

Parenting is a full-time job for which most parents have had little training. I want to share with you my faith and my understanding of the child: how she grows, develops, learns, thinks, and comes to know God.

As a parent, I often wished that I could wear a sign that said, "Off duty." Especially did I want to wear it at times when I was not setting the right example. I wanted to say, "Don't look at me now; don't listen to what I am saying because I am not being a good example for you." But you are never off duty, sign or no sign. You are always teaching. You cannot *not teach*. How sobering!

I trust that you will find this a practical guide as you increase in your own Christian faith and as you share your faith with your child. The first chapter reveals the importance of guiding your child toward God during these formative years. Chapters 2—7 help you know your child—what you can expect of him, what he needs along with what he can learn about God, and what you can do to guide him toward God. The last chapter challenges your commitment to your most important job.

Come with me on a developmental journey with your child from birth to six. What greater blessing and challenge can you have than that of guiding your child toward God during these crucial years?

Teach a child how he should live, and he will remember it all his life (Prov. 22:6, GNB).

1

The Importance
of the First Five Years

A beaming father presses his face against the window of a hospital nursery. He looks at his newborn son. Emotions are high. He is grateful to God for this child who is flesh of his flesh and that of his beloved wife. Nothing but the best is worthy for his child. He turns to his pastor with the sincere question, "Pastor, when should I start teaching Nathan about God?"

"You can begin now. It is never too early to nurture your child in the faith. You can begin by being a godly example of love. You will represent God to Nathan as he grows in his understanding of who God is. Surround your child with the realities of your own Christian faith. This is the best way to begin teaching Nathan about God."

Quietly, the pastor touched the father on the shoulder, and they paused to bow in prayer for the miracle of life and the wisdom to guide Nathan at home and at church.

In front of them lay Nathan, red, soft, crying—becoming adjusted to life outside his mother's warm womb. A new life, rich with possibilities, has been cast into the world. The world will never be the same again. Nathan is here. He has entered time and eternity.

The Miracle of Life

Miracle of miracles—life! Life began in the mind of God. "God said, 'Let Us [Father, Son, and Holy Spirit] make mankind in Our image, after Our likeness" (Gen. 1:26, AMP). Every baby that is born is part of that long succession of life from the beginning when God made human beings a part of divine creation.

God is the source of all life. At the moment of fertilization, the twenty-three chromosomes of the sperm and the twenty-three chromosomes of the egg mix and separate into pairs. These twenty-three pairs of the forty-six chromosomes give the child his genetic makeup. God's design for that life has been set. The pattern of his inheritance is laid.

Life indeed is a miracle—a sacred trust from God. A child's spiritual journey begins before birth. Each person is made in the image of God. Each person bears God's imprint. How exciting! Each human being is endowed with intelligence: the ability to think, reason, and choose. Each becomes accountable to his Creator for his words and actions. Each is dependent upon God for his fulfillment in life and his eternal destiny.

Your child is a designer's original. There never has been, nor is, nor ever shall be another person in the world exactly like your child. She is unique—one of a kind. Your glorious opportunity, privilege, and responsibility is to help her become what God made her able to become. What a joy to be able to guide your child during the years when your influence is the greatest, and your child is the most impressionable!

A child's heredity through the genes of his parents sets some limits and establishes potential. Heredity determines the body build, sex, mental capacity, and the color of skin, eyes, and hair. His environment or surroundings will have the greatest effect during these periods of rapid growth.

Crucial Beginnings

The first six years of life are the most important of all in the total development of your precious child, a gift from God. Foundations are laid for a lifetime. A foundation is crucial to the life of a building. The first six years are crucial to the building of a child's life. What your child becomes during his first five years largely determines the kind of person he will be for a lifetime. During the first and most important year of life, a child develops a sense of trust or lack of trust in himself and others. His basic outlook on life is established. Burton L. White in *The First Three Years of Life* notes that by age two, a child's competence can be predicted. Competence has to do with the child's feeling of self-confidence and willingness to attempt a task. At age three, the way a child will get along with other people can be predicted. A child's personality and self-concept (what he thinks of himself) are so established by age five that on the basis of these, you can predict his success in school, adolescence, marriage, and vocation.

The spiritual qualities developed during the first year of life will live on as the child moves through his childhood, youth, and adult years. The beginnings of life are powerful. They can start a child on the right road and free the child to become what God made him able to become, or they can start him on the wrong road and prevent him from becoming the unique person God made him to be.

God's Design for Growth

The child grows and develops as one personality; however, the child is complex in his nature. All parts of his being—the physical, social, emotional, mental, moral, and spiritual—affect every other part of him. To understand the child's total development, it is important to look at one part at a time.

Growth refers to what can be seen readily which has to do largely with physical size and body changes in height and weight. These are easily measured.

The child develops in a predictable way. The child develops in the direction from his head to his feet and from the center of his body to the extremities of his body. Development refers to the more subtle, less noticeable changes in the child. For example, we say the child is developing trust. To reach this conclusion, the parent notices certain behaviors in the child. Such behaviors might be: (1) The child stops crying when you pick him up. He trusts that you can comfort him. (2) Later he stops crying when he hears your approaching footsteps. He trusts that help is on its way.

For a child to function effectively, all parts of his being must develop and work together in harmony.

A child's personality represents the total of how each part of him affects every other part and how the total parts relate to the people and things in his world. The personality is shaped by what a child is at birth. He has a unique physical body, mental capacity, and temperament (disposition).

A child's inborn capacity affects the way he interacts with the people, objects, and events in his world, making him one of a kind. No other person in all the world is born with the same body structure and capacities, nor will any other have the same experiences. Even if twins or brothers and sisters have the same parents and live in the same house, they have different environments. Each child responds differently to each parent's care. The way each child responds to the parent's care will affect how the parent cares for the child. Some children are easier to care for than others. Some are colicky and fretful; others have little pain, enjoy cuddling, and are easy to care for.

Mileposts

Each child grows according to a predictable pattern of mileposts. Mileposts are periods of life which have noticable characteristics. The stages are sequential; that is, each follows the other. Just as physical growth and development occur in stages, so do mental, social, emotional, and moral and spiritual development. While the mileposts are predictable, your child will go through each milepost at his own rate of development. Some children develop quickly, and others slowly. But each child grows toward maturity. Growth and development are dynamic; that is, ever changing. Yesterday's child is not the same today. He is different because of the changes that have occurred in all areas of his development. No two babies follow exactly the same timing in all areas.

So what you read here are only general guidelines. A wide range of growth and development can be normal.

During these six years the child grows physically from total dependence to remarkable independence (much on her own), from acting on reflex and instinct to acting from learning.

Socially, she develops from not knowing that she is even a person to learning how to get along with other people cooperatively.

Emotionally, she moves from crying to communicate her feelings to a person who can use many expressions along with words to communicate feelings. Also, she can recognize happiness, sadness, and anger in the face of another and has a measure of control over her own emotions.

Mentally, the child changes from responding by instinct to learning by discovery. She has learned to speak to identify and communicate her needs, to converse, to imagine. She is an avid learner.

Morally and spiritually, the child has grown from no knowledge of God to a knowledge that God is a person most like the important persons in her life. She is developing a conscience, a sense of right and wrong, based on your example and upon what you have allowed her to do and what you have stopped her from doing.

How the Child Develops Spiritually

God is the designer of how a child grows, develops, learns, and thinks. God conformed Himself to His own laws of human growth and development. He became man and dwelled among us in the form of Jesus. Little is known of Jesus' childhood. Luke summarizes His childhood in these words, "And Jesus increased in wisdom [mentally] and stature [physically], and in favour with God [spiritually] and man [socially] (Luke 2:52). Each child follows the same pattern of growth and grows in the same areas as did Jesus. Each child grows physically, mentally, spiritually, and socially.

I believe that Jesus grew as children today grow and develop —that He grew in His love for God and people, and that He came to the age when He became accountable to God. According to Jewish custom, He became responsible as a man at or about the age of twelve. The child and the way he develops has been the object of many studies. Not surprisingly, that which we have discussed thus far is in keeping with this Jewish custom, that a child at or about the age of twelve moves into the last of the four stages of thinking as described by Jean Piaget, a Swiss psychologist.

1. The first stage is that of the child from birth until about two years of age when the child's thinking is based on the experi-

ences she has with her senses, and the control she gains over her physical body. (She thinks with the bits and pieces of information which are taken into her mind by what she sees, hears, tastes, smells, and feels with her body and with her emotions. Her increasing control over her body, first the use of her head, puts her in new positions to take in the sights and sounds. As she learns to use her body to move into space, she makes numerous discoveries. As the arms, hands, fingers, legs, feet, and toes become coordinated, she becomes an energetic explorer, learning about herself and the world around her.)

2. During the second stage from about two years until six or seven, the child is in a stage of limited thinking during which she does not think logically but thinks according to what she sees.

3. During the third stage from about seven through twelve, the child is logical but needs something tangible with which to think. For example: If you ask a child who is darkest of three people or to place three people in a row from lightest to darkest, he can work the problem if he has people to put in a row. However, if you say: "Sally is lighter than Jenny and darker than Jane. Who is darkest?" he would have a difficult time coming up with an answer.

4. At the last stage of thinking from about twelve years of age on, a person can think abstractly and can answer the question about Sally, Jenny, and Jane without having them present.

All aspects of a child's development affect his spiritual development. Guiding a child's spiritual development needs to take into account that the child is active by nature. Sitting for long periods of time is as inappropriate for preschoolers as having adults stand for a long period of time. God who made us knew that children needed to be taught spiritual truths throughout the day. He allowed for their active nature.

A five-year-old was asked what she learned following the Sunday School session. She answered, "Nothing."

"What do you mean 'nothing?' I brought you here to learn about God. Why didn't you learn something?"

"'Cause all we did was sit," was the child's reply.

This child associates learning with *doing* something *active*, being actively involved. Whatever happened that morning was inappropriate from the child's point of view.

Let us take clues from young children about their needs to learn. God has made them eager, curious, and engrossed with a need to know. We can be partners with God when we know God's design. God made each of us to be learners for a lifetime. What causes us to lose the enthusiasm of the child? The child is fascinated with life. He is born into a world of which he knows nothing, and he wants to know about all of it. During these moments of inquiry when he constantly asks "Why?" or "What's this?" he needs caring, understanding parents who will take the time to give spiritual meaning to answers he desires. He needs parents who encourage his questions and his search. God has made each of us with much more potential than we ever use. We are responsible and accountable for using our body, mind, and spirit to the fullest for His glory.

Isaiah, in foretelling the coming of the Lord and His reign in the hearts of men, said, "a little child shall lead them" (Isa. 11:6). The period of childhood was designed by God. No child should be deprived of this special time in life. Jesus used little children to teach adults what they should be like. In fact, adults are instructed to become as little children instead of teaching little children to become as adults. If we want them to become like we are, we need first to become like them. Ponder the words of Jesus for what you should become and what your child is like. "Verily, I say unto you, Except ye be converted, and become as little children, ye shall not enter into the kingdom of heaven. Whosoever therefore shall humble himself as this little child, the same is greatest in the kingdom of heaven" (Matt. 18:3-4).

The Role of the Parent

Jesus spoke about the relationship of the adult to a little child, "And whoever receives one such child in My name receives Me" (Matt. 18:5, NASB). Jesus said, "Let the children come to me and do not stop them, because the Kingdom of heaven belongs to such as these" (Matt. 19:14, GNB). What is Jesus saying here about the moral condition of little children? We are asked to let them come to Jesus, not forbid them. But what is meant by this? "Coming to Jesus" in this situation did not mean coming to Jesus in life commitment. Notice the example of what Jesus did when the children came to Him. He put his hands on them and prayed (Matt. 19:13). Then He let them go to do those things children do. He did not burden them with facts they could not understand. If we follow the example of Jesus, we are to touch them in love and pray for them. We are not to hinder them.

Jesus is no longer present in bodily form for parents to bring their children to. Parents are told, however, "Inasmuch as ye have done it unto one of the least of these my brethren, ye have done it unto me" (Matt. 25:40). How humbling! What we do to little children, we do to Jesus. What would you do to Jesus? How would you treat Him if He were alive today? You treat Jesus each day as you treat your child.

Follow the lead of the child in his need to know. Listen to the questions he asks. Notice when he is attempting to solve a problem or appreciating something in God's world.

Remember, your child does not think logically. However, the way a child thinks and learns makes sense to him. As adults who have the ability to think logically, we often try to use facts and content in an orderly way. If a child thought logically, he could never believe in Santa Claus (one man who delivered presents to all the boys and girls in a single night riding in a sleigh driven by flying reindeer). In fact, he would question flying reindeer. Each child is different, even at the same age and stage. Each has different needs with respect to learning.

If you recall the teachings of Jesus, He often taught after a question was asked. Thus, He met the needs of the listeners.

Jesus responded to those sent by John the Baptist who inquired, "Art thou he that should come? or look we for another?" (Luke 7:20). A lawyer asked, "Master, what shall I do to inherit eternal life?" (Luke 10:25). Jesus answered with questions: "What is written in the law? how readest thou?" (Luke 10:26). Again the lawyer questioned, "And who is my neighbour?" (Luke 10:29).

Sometimes we are tempted to teach little children all we know when we are not willing to learn what we are ready to learn ourselves. Jesus did not teach adults all He knew. Paul speaks to this when he said, "I have fed you with milk, and not with meat: for hitherto ye were not able to bear it, neither yet now are ye able" (1 Cor. 3:2). The amazing truth is that we have access to God's Holy Word. God yields its treasures to us as we give ourselves to seeking with all our hearts, and when we strive to do what it says. The Bible will never be conquered. The time will never come when you and I cannot learn more of its deeper meaning for our lives. The more I know, the more I want to know what God has in store for me through His precious Word.

Near the end of His earthly ministry, Jesus attempted to prepare His disciples for His tribulation and imminent death. He wanted them to know that He must go away, and afterward the Comforter would come. As he was telling them why He must go, He said, "I have yet many things to say unto you, but ye cannot bear them now" (John 16:12).

Jesus referred to adults as "little children" in Matthew 18:3. Was He referring to their relationship to him? Or was He speaking to their limited understanding of what He was saying about what He must endure? Even Peter did not understand what He meant when He said He was going away because Peter asked to go with Him.

What Can a Child Learn?

While children at these early ages have some of the same characteristics, what each needs to learn on a given day is determined by a child's unique experience. As Galileo said, "I cannot teach you anything, I can only help you discover it in yourself." When a child has a need to discover, that is the best time to learn. When your child wants to do what you are doing in the kitchen is the best time for you to encourage him to help. Mack wanted to work like his mother. Mother pulled a chair beside her near the cabinet and let Mack pull the lettuce apart and break off pieces for the salad. True, this took longer than if she had done it herself, but this was the opportune moment to follow the lead of a child. While slower, this was good economy of time. Mack is learning that he is a person with respect. He feels important because he can help; he can do it himself. His mother can use this natural situation to share a Bible thought. "Mack, thank you for helping Mother. The Bible says, 'Help one another.' You have helped Mother by pulling the lettuce apart to help make the salad." Then she softly sang, "I am glad God gave you hands so you can help make salad."

This lesson in helping and thanking God for hands was spontaneous. What Mack learned was not built into a sequence of what he should learn on that particular day. But his mother knew about the "teachable moment," and she was prepared to say or sing the words which fit the actions. She knew that a child does not think independently of his experiences. She knew that he learns by association. He will have good feelings about his mother who lets him try what he wants to try. He will have good feelings about himself when he has some measure of success. Talking about Bible truths in isolation has little meaning. The child learns about Bible truths best when he can apply them to his life.

During the daily routine of life, many opportunities await your ability to sense your child's need to *do* and to *learn*. The natural occurrences of life can become the subjects of conversation which makes the Bible relevant. That is why at church, the learning areas in the preschool departments should relate to the meaningful everyday experiences of life so that the Bible can be taught, not in isolation but in association with real-life activities. The Bible is for living, not just for saying. We want every child to come to feel that the Bible is God's guide for living. The child learns through firsthand experiences. Along with these you can use Bible-related pictures, stories, songs, conversations, and prayers.

Bible stories should be carefully selected, and only the part which has meaning for the child should be used. Answer these questions prayerfully to evaluate a Bible story:

1. What do you want your child to learn from this story?

2. Does this story relate to something meaningful which the child is experiencing?

3. Does the Bible story keep the attention of the child?

4. Are the words understandable to the child?

5. Is the spiritual truth in the story clear?

Are Children Smarter?

Research studies show that preschoolers today are no smarter than they were over fifty years ago. When the Gesell tests administered in the 1930s were replicated, the results showed that their vocabularies are no greater today than prior to TV. Children's thinking is still limited and illogical. The language of preschoolers far exceeds their thinking, and we are often fooled by their language. They can talk about things they don't understand.

We are fooled into thinking that children are smarter because of television. What we fail to remember is that preschoolers learn best by doing and from firsthand experiences. Television provides neither. Preschoolers can say long and meaningless words. They can name all the dinosaurs, using long technical words. Do they really have a concept of a dinosaur? Do we? Science has already discovered that some of the things we have previously thought about dinosaurs have been proven false.

A Variety of Experiences Needed

Young children learn spiritual concepts through many, many experiences. Facts are easy to learn and easy to forget. Facts unused are lost to memory. Learning unused is learning abused. Preschoolers only learn what has meaning for them from the Bible stories, verses and thoughts, songs, pictures, and conversation. We are not always teaching what we think we are teaching. Sometimes we think because we say it, children learn it. Would that learning were so easy! The big ideas about the Bible and its truths are learned through many and varied experiences. As the child matures, he is better able to grasp the deeper spiritual meanings. Think of the basic concepts which you want your child to learn. You want him to know about God and to experience God. He will learn about God little by little. At first God will be a name he hears a loving parent say. Later he will learn that God is a person most like the important people in his life. Then he will learn that God loves him and made many things for him to enjoy and use. Later he will learn that God sent Jesus to show us He loved us. His understanding of God will grow throughout a lifetime.

Preschoolers have difficulty knowing what God made and what people made. Because we know, we take for granted that anyone knows that God made the flowers and other things. Do you know the difference between a man-made and a God-made lake? Can you describe it to a young child?

A concept which we hope children will gain an increasing understanding of is that of sharing. Preschoolers have a difficult time sharing. Some adults do also. What have you shared lately that was of real value to you? Preschoolers don't share readily because of the way they think. They are self-centered. This is not the same as selfish. This means that they have only one view of things—*theirs.* They cannot put themselves in the place of another, think from that point of view, and respond according to the need they discover. Adults have the capacity to see from another's point of view but often fail to do so. When adults are self-centered, they are selfish. They have more than one view, and they still choose theirs. A child is not selfish because he has only *one* view; therefore, he has no choice.

Can Children Share?

The concept of sharing begins at birth when a parent gives love and physical care to the child. A child learns how good it feels to receive. The child who has experienced the joy of receiving wants to share. At about eight months a child will give up a toy to another person for a moment. Thank her. Say:

"Rhonda, you gave me your key chain. Thank you. Now you want it back. Here it is." Notice a child's every attempt to give up or take turns with her toy. This is a prerequisite to sharing. Real sharing is giving up something which is yours for keeps.

You can teach a child to say, "Share with one another." He will need, however, repeated opportunities to share and hear the Bible thought before he learns the meaning and joy of sharing. This particular Bible thought also illustrates another concern. Some parents think that a child should learn Bible verses just as they are in the Bible.

If this verse were quoted from the King James Version, a child would hear, "That they do good, that they be rich in good works, ready to distribute, willing to communicate" (1 Tim. 6:18). What would a child learn having heard these words? Remember, he learns what has meaning to him. Bible thoughts are used to put the meaning of the verse into words which the child can understand.

Just as you attempt to explain something to a child by putting it in words he can understand, you would want to do this to Bible words so the child could get meaning from them. Is that not what your pastor does when he preaches? He reads a Scripture passage, then he interprets it, and shares ways it speaks to us today. You might interpret it to mean, "Give what you have to others." Do we really want our children to learn to share? When your child gives away a toy which you have just paid for, do you commend her or reprimand her? When your child grows older and loans her new bicycle to a friend, do you commend her or say, "Why did you do that? You know he will probably wreck it before he gets back?" We need to think about our own example of sharing. This may also be an area in which you can learn from your child.

No task in life is quite so humbling and awesome as is that of guiding your child toward God. You are accountable for your child's spiritual development until the child becomes accountable before God. Your child will learn mostly from your example. During the years, therefore, when your child is most impressionable, you are his guide. I pray for you as you accept with humility and joy the challenge which is yours—to instruct your child in the way God made him to grow, develop, think, and learn, and according to his own God-given gifts and potential.

It is never too early to start guiding your child toward God. You are to teach her at her level of readiness and understanding and according to her abilities—that means not too little and not too much. I pray that God will give you the wisdom to know what and when your child is ready to learn.

You Teach What You Are

If you are courteous, considerate, and respectful, your child learns to be kind.

If you are generous, caring, thoughtful, your child learns to be giving.

If you are attentive to his needs, he becomes thoughtful of others.

If you are kind spoken and loving, he learns to be gentle.

If you notice his attempts to succeed and cheer him on, he becomes self-confident.

If you are loud, angry, easily upset, he becomes hostile and irritable.

If you value your worth, he learns to feel worthwhile.

If you are Godlike, your child learns to love God.

If you love your child unconditionally, your child learns to love like God loves.

I am fearfully and wonderfully made (Ps. 139:14).

2
The First Year: Developing Trust

Who can resist a newborn baby? A man and a woman who are Christians but who drifted away from church after marriage find that with their firstborn they want their baby to have the best start in life. Nothing can keep them from striving for the best. Their hearts are more tender then than ever. This miracle of life is present with them. Each time that little warm body is snuggled close to theirs, they feel in touch with God and his beautiful design. They want to become the best possible parents for this child who is totally dependent on their guidance.

What to Expect of Your Child

How you care for a child's physical needs affects every part of his being. As you feed him when he is hungry, you are nourishing his soul. He feels safe and secure with you, the person upon whom he depends. When you talk lovingly to him as you feed him, you are challenging his mind and feeding his emotions.

When you talk to Eric and wait for his response and when you allow him to take a turn in the "conversation," you are helping lay the basic mental structures of his mind. He is learning his name and how to communicate. His spirit is nurtured. He is getting positive feelings about himself, the people around him, and his world.

When a child's spirit is nurtured, his physical body is affected. A child thrives physically when he is encouraged with loving care and your voice. He is motivated to gain skills in the use of his body.

A child who has only his physical needs met may lose mental potential and lose the will to live. Babies who are only diapered and fed begin to waste away physically and emotionally. Affectionate human contact, gentle touches, and calm soft talk are the vital ingredients in a child's will to become fully human. A child can lose mental ability within a few days after birth if he is not stimulated with human nurture—cuddled, patted, touched, talked to, and received eye contact.

Not so long ago the question of whether to breast- or bottle-feed was not so important. The main concern then was whether or not the baby would have the needed body and eye contact with the parent. Now, however, some advantages are emerging for breast feeding which relate to the child's immunity to certain diseases and allergies. Whether you breast- or bottle-feed, however, please cuddle the baby so he feels the security and comfort of your body contact, sees you looking into his eyes with intimate love, and hears you talk to him expecting him to respond.

You may wish to continue a career and will be faced with choosing quality child care. Choose someone who will respect your child's uniqueness; someone who will help your child feel loved and who has similar values to yours. A book, such as *How to Choose and Use Child Care* compiled by Jean Kirk Reynolds (Broadman), may be helpful.

Other caregivers are not substitutes for parents. They supplement the child's care and support the parents. A child knows who his parents are and who cares for him.

At birth you will find that your child can move all the parts of his tiny body. His body works! Some babies are more active than others. Some appear to be more fragile than others. But somehow they don't break easily.

Your baby will be different from all the other babies in the whole world. And every baby you have will be different from all the other babies you have had. You can judge their differences on several characteristics. Just ask these questions to assess your child's uniqueness.

1. How active is your child?
2. What kind of temperament does he have?
3. How long is his attention span?
4. How strongly (with what intensity) does he respond?
5. How flexible is he?
6. What gets his interest?
7. How persistent is he?
8. What kind of rhythm or schedule does he have?
9. How easily distracted is he?

Get in touch with your baby and what he is like based on these characteristics. Then you will be able to give him better instruction conformable to his unique bent and gifts.

Babies come into the world eager to learn. They are sight hungry. A newborn searches his environment. He is sound hungry. He will turn his head to the high-pitched voice of his mother whose voice he seems to recognize at birth. He will turn his head to his father's voice if Father speaks with a high pitch.

God made each baby with an inborn capacity to thrive, to grow, and to develop his unique potential. In this small dependent body lies the potential for greatness. Only God knows his special gifts.

Birth to Three Months

While lying on her back, a baby turns her head from side to side. Notice her usual positions. When she lies on her back and turns her head to the left side, you will notice her left arm extend and her right arm bent upward at the elbow.

She hears, remember? Sudden noises alarm. She may stiffen, flail her arms, and cry.

Her nervous system will be adjusting to the outside world at this time. She may awaken crying from her sleep. She may sneeze and cough.

Although she has little muscle control, she may be able to lift her head when lying on her stomach. When you hold her without support to the head, her head may fall forward.

Her fingers are usually clinched, but she has an automatic grasp. Watch her fingers tighten as you let her hold yours.

She is sight hungry. Her eye muscles are most active. Watch as she hears a bell making a sound.

She sleeps a lot but not at one stretch. She awakens often.

Your child is born with a temperament. She will be happy, easygoing, relaxed, outgoing or irritable, withdrawn, hard to please. Some are sparklers; others are quiet, uptight, demanding, moody, or passive.

Her mouth is used for more than food. It is an instrument for scientific discovery. Your child arrives knowing how to suck and swallow, drool, hiccup, cough, and goo. (She may even suck her thumb before she is born.)

During her first month, you will notice that the action is with the head. She lifts her head briefly when held in a sitting position and turns it from side to side. Soft talk, singing, and rocking are soothing.

During the second month, put her on her stomach over your

knee and watch her hold her head up to the level of her body. You have waited for the time when your child could hold one of the toys she received before birth. Now she can hold one—for about ten seconds.

You will recognize that she is learning. She can now recognize her eating position. When you hold her in that position, she starts sucking, lunchtime or not. Hopefully she is now sleeping better although she will be awake longer.

And now the time you have waited for so eagerly has arrived. Your child has become more interested in the world around her. She will smile back and coo. How rewarding! You can enjoy watching her blow bubbles.

Bright-colored objects fascinate her, and she will probably follow their movements from side to side. Place mobiles over her crib eight or nine inches above her eyes.

Three to Six Months

From three to six months your child happily responds to your playfulness. He will laugh out loud at your antics. A distinct personality is emerging. He smiles when he sees you.

From now until the tenth month, you will see great leaps in mental development. Great effort is expended to learn how to get what he sees and wants.

As fingers become toys, you will see him put his hands together. He likes to be pulled into a sitting position.

He begins to pat the bottle or the breast while nursing. He discovers his toes. Bathtime becomes fun.

Now he can use syllables (sounds) to get your attention. Looking in a mirror causes him to smile.

When he hears footsteps, he gets excited. He can now imitate you by coughing, laughing, and sniffing (a flower).

By around seven months, place an object in front of him and

watch him get into action. He can now roll from back to tummy and hold onto some objects.

Six to Nine Months

From six to nine months, your child may be able to sit alone—well, at least for a moment. With support, she might sit for thirty minutes. And just listen to her talk!

Her new ability to creep gives a sense of power. Heretofore, she depended on you to get everything for her. Now she can do some things for herself. What a milestone!

By around eight months your child is curious. She wants to check out everything. And now that she can crawl, she will. The big problem is: she does not know what is harmful.

Eating becomes more enjoyable. If your baby uses a bottle, do not leave her alone with it even though she can hold it herself.

She may change from sitting to lying down. She may enjoy standing if she has something sturdy to hold to.

Now it is game time. Your baby is more and more able to interact with you. She lets you know when she wants you near.

Somewhere between five and eight months your child reaches a mental milestone. She recognizes the difference between a parent's face and the face of a stranger. This frequently is referred to as stranger anxiety. You may start saying: "My child has reached a mental milestone. She now knows the difference between my face and that of a stranger."

By now your child knows her name. She also knows by the sound of your voice whether you approve or disapprove of what she does.

At or about nine months your child can sit with ease. She tries to stand and may pull up by herself. Proud of her new ability to stand by herself, she suddenly learns that she does not know how to sit down. She does know how to cry for help.

She now can use her index finger and thumb together.

A new mental ability surfaces. She learns cause and effect. She knows to pull a string (the cause) attached to a toy to retrieve a toy (the effect).

Keep on talking to your child about what she is doing. Use words which she will be learning first. Name the actual things she is experiencing. You may "read" one or two pictures from a book as your child shows interest.

Give your child freedom to move about. That means that playpens and infant seats would be used only occasionally.

Nine to Twelve Months

From nine until twelve months, toys that challenge a child's skills are: nesting and stacking toys, large soft balls, containers for filling and dumping, dolls with painted features and painted hair, containers with lids, telephone, and jack-in-the-box-type toys.

This is the time to start making simple requests: "Bring Daddy the book." You can also give commands. "Give Mommy the pencil" (or some unsafe object). Commands are really requests which you expect the child to learn to comply with.

Check your child's emotional and mental health by asking these questions:

● During the first two months, does your child search with his eyes when there are things to see and sounds to hear?

● From two to four months, does your child enjoy playing with you? That is, does he respond with giggles and motions that say "more"?

● Between four and six months, does your child carry on a

conversation with you? That is, does he respond to your sounds by making some sounds?

• By age twelve months, do you notice your child imitating the things you do ("talking" on a telephone, waving bye-bye)?

Were you able to answer each question with a *yes?*

Your Child's Needs

You look at that irresistible, small face and body and think— how helpless, how fragile! She is not helpless. She can let you know when she needs something. And she will! She is not fragile —she has an incredible ability to survive.

Your child comes marvelously equipped at birth to command your attention. But she does not come with instructions. You have to decide what she needs when she is crying. She comes with a loud alarm system.

Soon you will be able to distinguish her cries. Her cries may signal hunger, discomfort, or boredom. The discomfort may be caused by gas pains, soiled diapers, from being too hot or too cold, or from being in the same position for too long. She mostly communicates through crying but by the end of the first month, she will be making other noises which you will learn to detect.

Her cry is your command. Honor it. She needs your help and is telling you her needs in the only way she knows how. Crying is God's plan for getting the two of you together. When you respond to her pleas for help she learns that she can depend on you to meet her needs and can trust you in her time of need. The groundwork is being laid for trust to grow. She is learning to feel valuable.

Your child needs to be handled frequently. Get comfortable holding your child. You can't spoil her during the the first year of life! Actually, when you meet her needs upon demand during the first year of your life, your child gains a sense of trust in you and will be more independent during the second year of life. So hold her as much as you like. And, of course, only as much as she likes.

Handle her by placing her in different positions so that she can see the world from many different views.

Your eyes are very special to your child. When he is in the nursing position (if you are attentive to him), he is looking you in the eye and you are looking into his. Eyes are the window to the soul. Generous amounts of intimate eye contact feed a child's spirit, and in turn his body thrives.

Physical affection is vital to your child's emotional, mental, and spiritual health. Hold her cheek to cheek, kiss her on the cheek, hug her gently, pat her easily. She can sense your love.

Ross Campbell in his book *Do You Really Love Your Child?* mentions that little girl babies under a year of age are shown five times more physical affection than little boys the same age. Could this be why boys from three through adolescence frequent psychologists and psychiatrists' clinics five times more than girls? Both boys and girls need abundant physical affection during this first year.

Each child needs to have toys and activities to match his present and emerging skills. During the first six weeks, place bright-colored objects (larger than five inches) about a foot above the baby's eyes and move the objects slowly above the child's head.

From six weeks until about three-and-a-half months, your baby will enjoy watching a brightly colored object moving over his head from one side to another. Let his eyes focus on the object, then move it slowly and watch him track it.

If a face is so important to a child, see what he does when he sees his own face in the mirror. Put him on his stomach for at least a half hour per day so that he can exercise from that position. At times prop him in an infant seat.

Music is soothing and stimulating and so is talk if such is used at a low volume.

A special relationship with the mother develops. We call this bonding or attachment. This feeling grows out of dependency nurtured with love.

From about three-and-a-half months until about five-and-a-half months, your child will enjoy crib toys to kick and to reach for. A cradle gym at her feet, to which you have placed her foot that caused a jingle of the bell, will entice her to try to make the sound again. Words can encourage her.

At eight months feed the child's fascination for small objects by providing her with safe, small (not small enough to swallow) objects for holding, dropping, and banging. Play peekaboo, pat-a-cake, and hide-and-seek. Playful now with familiar persons, she enjoys these social games. She can also wave bye-bye.

From nine to twelve months, your child may be walking. At any rate, you will see that he has good coordination of legs and feet as well as fingers. He discovers many things he can do with a toy—hold it, shake it, take it apart, put it with or into something else.

At this age he is highly social. He will give his toy to you (if only for a moment).

While his mouth is still used to discover objects, he can use his eyes and hands better to check things out.

A budding individual develops as he becomes aware that he can move away from you as well as toward you.

Preferences are well defined. He knows what he wants and what he does not want. He is persistent in getting what he wants. He may even push you out of his way.

Crawling and walking can get him into unexplored space. He

can climb up the stairs, and he can fall down them. His mind has grown—he can solve problems.

He is a great imitator. What he sees, he tries. He can fill and dump objects, push a toy, rock the baby, hit a spoon against a box, unwrap a box, scribble with crayons, remove a shoe-box lid, make sounds as if he is in a great conversation, look at pictures in a book, hug, kiss, pat, drink from a cup, pick up his food, and many more things.

You are his benchmark of safety. He needs to know you are close by. When he gets into trouble, he will come to you.

What Your Child Learns About God

Your child learns before he is born. We have known for some-time that a mother's emotions can affect her unborn child. When she gets upset, her body releases hormones which get to the baby in the same way the mother feeds the baby. Now research states that your baby can see, hear, and feel before he is born. If his senses take in information, he can learn in the womb. How can a child see before he is born when he is growing inside a womb inside the mother's abdomen? To better understand how this is possible, close your eyes and ask some-one to turn the lights on or off. Can you tell the difference? A baby is sensitive in somewhat the same way to light and dark-ness.

The expectant mother can hear a loud noise of a truck passing by and will not jump when she hears it. But the fetus gets excited and becomes active when the mother hears the noise. The touch of Mother's hand on the abdomen and the sound of her voice are comforting. This new discovery leads me to be-lieve that a mother and father can pass on something of their quiet, assuring faith to their child.

By the end of the first year your child will understand more than he can communicate. Your young baby is highly sensitive to your emotions and tone of voice. You are his source of comfort. Your presence is soothing when you are relaxed, calm, and soft-spoken. Warm, loving contact or closeness with another human body and the sound of a familiar voice nurture his trust in your loving care.

The most significant spiritual qualities are developed during infancy. Trust is born of dependency on the part of the baby whose needs are supplied upon demand with tender care by the one upon whom the child depends. Thus, dependency and compassion combine to give birth to trust.

During the first and most important year, the child acquires a basic outlook on life. Life is either good or bad, pleasant or unpleasant, happy or unhappy, satisfying or frustrating, optimistic or pessimistic.

During the first three months, a child becomes attached to the person who cares for her. A bond of trust has developed when a child shows that she feels greater comfort with the one who gives her most of her care. This attachment or bonding of the baby to the parent can be likened to our dependent relationship with God, trusting Him for life itself in the here and now and for eternity.

The loving relationship of a dependent child and compassionate parents lays the foundation for the child's first attitude toward God, the Father.

Before a child can learn about God, she needs to become acquainted with who you are and who she is. Your child who loves and trusts you will have warm feelings about the word *God* when you say it because she has warm feelings about you. A loving relationship of parent and child is the foundation for discipline. Discipline is teaching. A child wants to learn from someone she loves. So, at first, your child gets an attitude about the person whose hands touch and feed her and whose voice and footsteps soothe and give hope. This attitude provides a beginning for her concept of God.

As Lisa hears you lovingly say or sing, "I love you, Lisa. (You use *your* child's name.) And God loves you, too," God will be just a name she hears. As she becomes more aware of you as a person, she will have mental images and feelings with which to associate the name *God* with a person who does kind things. God becomes more than a name. The foundation is laid for thinking of God as a person.

Give your child many opportunities to experience the things God has made. Use words to help the child learn to label or name what he has experienced. When Mark feels the tickle of the grass as his bare feet press on it, say, "Grass. Mark's feet touch the grass. The grass tickles. God made the grass." Begin talking about God with your natural voice. You want your child to associate God with everyday experience. You are laying the foundation for him to think of God as personal and caring.

Everytime Mark has an experience with nature, you can help him feel good about himself as well as be more aware of God and what he made. When you say, "God gave Mark eyes so he can see the flower," Mark hears his name and through repeated experiences he learns what his eyes are for and what they can do.

Mark becomes more aware that God gave him a family each time you are with him. His new awareness begins as you use the names *Mother* and *Daddy* when you are doing something with and for him. "Mother is washing Mark's face." "Daddy is rocking Mark."

Notice every skill a child has developed. Talk about it when the child is using that skill. In this way, he learns that God made him to do many things. You might say, "Matthew can put the ball in the box. Look what Matthew can do. God gave Matthew hands so he can put the ball in the box." Matthew feels valuable and worthwhile.

As you show your love to people, Ann learns that people are valuable and worthwhile. As she watches you touch another baby gently, she, too, will learn to touch gently.

Matthew can also learn that at church he is happy (if he has happy experiences there). Hopefully, he will learn that people at church love him. The people at church let him turn the pages in the Bible. They show him pictures of Jesus and the children. They feed him, diaper him, hold him, sing to him, and talk to him about what they are doing. He hears his teachers sing, "I am happy. Matthew came to church."

How You Can Guide Your Child Toward God

A loving parent will make opportunities and use them to show love to the young child. Use the word *God* at times when you are giving affection. You pick Jeffrey up from his bed and hold him securely to your shoulder and say: "Jeffrey, Mommy loves you. Daddy loves you. And God loves you."

As you take him for a walk outside when he needs a new position or a change of scenery, sing a song about something God made which you are experiencing together. Help him see and touch the flower. Use a natural voice to sing or say, "God made the flower for Jason to see (touch, smell)."

All through the day, natural situations invite you to notice with your child what God has made and to thank God for it. When Sarah is nursing, say, "Sarah tastes the milk. Mmmmm, milk tastes so good. Thank you, God, for Sarah's milk."

As you hold Jason in your lap, show him the Bible. Touch the Bible gently as you say, "Bible. This is a Bible, Jason." Then turn to a picture of Jesus. Touch the picture and say, "Jesus. This is a picture of Jesus. Jesus loves Jason."

This is the time to start calling by name the things Jason sees. This is called labeling. You are teaching him that things have names.

Jason may not understand the words, but they can be among the first things he names or labels. You have just introduced him to the Bible, a book about Jesus. Jason enjoys special times with his mother or daddy. Looking at a book and seeing the pictures brings Jason and Mommy and Daddy together for moments of closeness.

If Jason sees a Bible only at church, he learns that the Bible is a special Book to be used at church. When Jason sees you use the Bible at home and at church and he has happy experiences with the Bible, he learns that the Bible is special to his parents at home and at church. Thus, he gets a foundation for the importance of this special Book.

The Bible should be used while you are with the child, lest he tear the pages. You can lovingly teach him to turn the pages gently. To attract Jason to the Bible, you might place a leaf on the opened Bible at a picture of Jesus sitting outdoors. Say, "God made the leaves for Jason to see. Jesus liked to see the leaves." Then you may want to take Jason outside and let him experience the leaves in their natural setting. His mind is taking in new information through his senses—his eyes, ears, nose, mouth, and skin. His spirit and emotions are being fed with loving care. When he is emotionally satisfied, learning is a joy.

As you hold Heather's body next to yours and hug her gently, kissing her on the cheek, say, "I love you, Heather. God (Jesus) loves Heather, too." Heather associates words with actions. As she experiences love, she hears the word *God* or *Jesus* and develops warm feelings about these words. Heather's name is her label, the word by which she is known. For that reason, I recommend that you call a child's name when she is doing that which is appropriate. Then she will associate her name with positive feelings about herself. If you call her name mostly to correct her, she may associate her name with negative feelings about herself.

As Lindsey discovers her image in the stainless steel mirror say, "Lindsey. Lindsey sees her face in the mirror." Then you may feel like saying or singing (your own tune, of course), "God gave Lindsey eyes so she can see herself in the mirror." Lindsey learns that she is somebody special, and somebody Mother (Daddy) talks or sings about. She feels loved.

As Lindsey gets her first impressions of what God is like from her parents' care, she also gets impressions about what people are like. If she can trust you, she tends to trust other people. When she develops relationships with other caring people, you feel secure when you leave her with others.

You may have difficulty leaving your child, thinking that no one else will really care for her like you would. You may feel guilty for neglecting your duty to your child, thinking *My child is depending on me.* Or you may feel that you cannot bear to be separated from her. This feeling is the most difficult to handle. You may suffer more than your child. Both parent and child need some time apart. Think of this as your child's opportunity to experience love and attention from other persons who can become important people in her life. You need some relief from the consuming care which a young child demands. You need time to replenish your creative energies so that you can return to your child with a refreshing attitude, feeling able to cope with whatever comes next.

How important it is for your child to have happy experiences in his room at church! You want your child's first associations with church to be happy and satisfying. If your child goes regularly to Sunday School during the months prior to the period of stranger anxiety (around five months), he can become attached to his teachers who will be familiar to him at that time. Happy, caring, loving, and faithful teachers who prepare to teach each child individually can become significant persons in the life of your child. Everytime your child attends church, he is adding to his understanding of what *church* is. He is also learning that other people love him, that he is valuable and important, and that other important people talk about God and Jesus. Choose a church who values your child as a unique gift of God, born ready to learn and develop his God-given potential.

Parents, do not treat your children in such a way to make them angry. Instead, raise them with Christian discipline and instruction (Eph. 6:4, GNB).

3
The Second Year: Developing Independence

What to Expect of Your Child

Suddenly your child is no longer a baby. A distinct personality has emerged. Your child is becoming a person in her own right. To do so, she will assert her will. She has strong feelings about what she wants and does not want. Heretofore, your child was mostly dependent on you for her every need. You felt so useful being able to meet her needs. Now that your child is learning to be on her own, her need for you will be less. However, she may actually need you even more for her own protection. She can creep or crawl or walk. You work hard to encourage her to walk. Sometimes between nine to eighteen months she will. Then your world and hers will change.

This new ability gives the child a sense of power. She is now able to do for herself, to get where she wants to go, and to get what she wants. She insists on doing for herself. She may grab the spoon while you are feeding her. She may resist when you dress her.

During this time you watch your child move from one small step to the stage of space exploration. No longer can you leave her unsupervised. "She's into everything," you say. And that with vigor. You will find it trying on your patience and resources to keep up with her. The mouthing of objects soon disappears as she becomes obsessed with what she can do with her body in space and what she can explore with her fingers. She will let you chase her and will even hide so you can "find the baby." She enjoys being the center of attraction. Whatever she does that excites your smiles and applause, she continues to do.

Your child can understand more words than she can use. She can follow such simple directions as, "Show me your tongue." When she does not know the words to use to get what she wants, she will point to show you. Later she will take your hand and walk you to what she wants.

Your child is a relentless learner. He works at walking—like a runner practices for an Olympic event. His undaunted effort should not be intruded upon with attempts to toilet train. When his body is desperate to move, is no time to try to get him to sit on the toilet. Also, when he gives his major energy to walking, do not expect too much talking. An early walker may delay talking. An early talker may delay walking.

Just watch him grow! He can now wave bye-bye when you ask him to, and you no longer have to show him how. When he hears words, he has mental images of their meaning. He enjoys "singing." Well, that is what a parent would call it. Others might call it making noise with the music. He will even offer a toy to the child in the mirror. That is a first attempt at sharing.

Your child enjoys playing ball. Sit on the floor and spread your legs and show her how to spread hers. Play the game "Roll the Ball." Say or sing, "Roll the ball to Elizabeth." When Elizabeth holds the ball, instruct her by saying or singing, "Roll the ball to Mommy (Daddy)."

This is the "I-can-do-it-myself" stage. She can undress herself and does so when you least expect it. A mother going to church recently found her toddler naked on the back seat of the car. She can take off better than she can put on. She can take off her shoes and socks. She can even feed herself (if you call feeding getting the food to her mouth anyway she can). She can work two- or three-piece jigsaw puzzles and put large pegs in a pegboard. This requires supervision.

The great imitator learns to laugh, talk on the telephone, make the sounds of animals, label (name) what he sees in pictures. He can point to the picture of the dog (cat) or whatever you have helped him experience. Also, he can name body parts, point to them, and point to the body parts of a doll.

About fifteen to eighteen months of age, your child is constant motion. He can be so helpful now. Whereas before he took things apart, now he can put them (well, some of them) together again.

He enjoys talking and saying many sounds in succession from which you can pick up an occasional real word. When he has had many experiences with an orange, a picture of an orange, and the word *orange,* he learns that the picture and the word represent the same idea. His memory is developing. When he sees a car in the yard, he may know if it is "Mother's car," "Daddy Paul's (Granddaddy's) car," or "Lonnie's (neighbor's) car."

She is developing many concepts. Anything round is called a ball. The water tower shaped like a ball is called "*big* ball." She enjoys carrying or wagging, a doll or favorite toy. She can give "sugar" or show affection to a toy. The kind of physical affection which you show her, she can imitate with you or the doll.

What joy to a parent when you hear your child hum or sing or dance spontaneously to the music! "She is *so* smart," you say.

She can put two words together to tell you what she wants, can sit still while you dress her, let you know when her pants are wet or soiled, lock her mouth or turn her head when she does not want to be fed, and can follow two directions such as: "Go to the chair. Bring Mommy the pillow."

He gets along more with other children toward the end of this year. Earlier, another child was a toy to be poked, pushed, bitten ("kissed"). Now he can play alongside of or near another child.

While his body is growing, provide many activities outside which he can choose for exercise—safe toys which he can push, pull, stack, fill, empty (dump), pull apart, put together, operate (turn a knob or dial to cause an immediate response such as louder volume or the ringing phone).

Physically your child is growing taller. As she loses her baby fat, she looks more like a child. Major changes occur in her mind. She relies less and less on trial and error and more and more on the mental images she has stored to figure out what will work and what does not. She now thinks to work a puzzle rather than just turning a part until it fits. She can also remember what she has seen you do and imitate it at a later time. She can "play ball" using a pretend bat. She can pretend to sweep the floor, dust the furniture, or wash the dishes. She can even let a wooden block be a car which she pushes with her hand while making spluttery car engine sounds.

What Your Child Needs

The second year of life—what a challenge! You will need all the energy and resourcefulness you can muster. Knowing the needs of your child will help you have the patience to meet hers. Your child needs to feel loved, safe, and secure. When these needs are met, she will be best able to master the developmental task of becoming independent and self-controlled.

Her main task is to learn how to walk and to run. This requires a safe space where she can practice with freedom and confidence. Your child needs to know that you care about her accomplishments. Applaud her attempts to walk.

Your child's body has a marvelous wisdom which dictates to the child when he is ripe to learn a new skill. You can assist or hinder by the environment which you provide. Let the child lead you in your understanding of his needs to discover. Watch him practice and attempt new things. Encourage with delight his successes. Do not pressure him to develop faster than he chooses.

While your child is becoming a person in his own right, he will assert himself and his will. Often his behavior is thought to be negative or defiant. He begins the lifelong task of choosing when to be independent (use his will) and when to be dependent (submit his will or conform to another's wishes or demands). From the child's point of view, his use of the word *no* is to let you know his likes and dislikes, what he wants to do and does not want to do. If his favorite word becomes *no,* just remember that he is practicing the new word which he has heard you say perhaps many times. How often have you said *yes yes* to him?

This is the time to toddlerproof your house or at least the room your explorer uses most of the time. Remove your valuables from his reach. Do not make your child responsible for them when he knows nothing of their value or what will happen when he handles them. Neither does he know what is hazardous or poison. You will eliminate much of your child's "misbehavior" which occurs when your toddler is faced with unreasonable temptations. Not only will you create a climate of freedom to explore in safety, but you will make life more pleasant and enjoyable for yourself. You can use the energy you would waste on keeping your child away from valuables on quality time with your child.

This is the stage of active exploration. With your house prepared with your child in mind, you will find your need to say *no no* less frequently. Too many times of saying no no and slapping of hands cause your child to withdraw from opportunities to discover. She will be unwilling to risk your punishment and displeasure. *No no* should be used at critical times when a child's safety is at stake. This will be needed sparingly if you have proofed your house and restricted areas of danger.

When the child continues his activity after you have said *no,* remove him from the temptation or remove the temptation. Your child is not yet at the age of reason. Distract him by saying: "Let's read a book." "Where is the dog?" "What does the dog say?" Or take the child to a window to see something outside or take him for a walk.

Your child is intrigued with his newfound skills of lugging, tugging, pushing, pulling, poking, punching, filling, dumping, hauling, and playing house. And don't forget throwing! Just remember the order in which he learns these. He dumps or empties before he learns to fill. That goes for wastebasket and dresser drawers, too.

Household items are as inviting, if not more so, than bought toys. You need not feel your child is deprived if you do not buy the latest and most expensive "child development" toys. Empty cardboard boxes of various sizes capture her attention. They afford an endless variety of creative uses. Cut off the top of a large cardboard box, turn it on one side, and she will crawl into it. She enjoys just pushing one across the floor. Other inviting items for learning are: pots and pans with covers, a coffeepot (no sharp spouts, please) with a basket to be dumped and reassembled (put together), plastic containers and lids, cardboard blocks (can be made out of shoe boxes with lids taped on and covered with contact paper to make more attractive), plastic or stainless steel mixing bowls that nest, small objects (too large to be swallowed) which can be used to put in and take out of the containers, outdated magazines, and numerous other items you will think of or your child will discover.

Your child feels secure knowing that things have places, and he now remembers where he put things. He may get upset or puzzled when something is not in its usual place. Use a toy shelf instead of a toy chest. Put out a few toys at a time. Add new toys occasionally, and remove the less popular ones.

The days are gone when the house is uncluttered. Your child enjoys scattering toys (that's what you call it). She takes a toy, sees something else more attractive, drops what she has to pick up another. After several decisions like this, the floor is covered. Make a game of putting the toys back in their places. You show her how and thank her for every time she puts them back. Clap your hands and say: "Jennifer, you put the doll back in its bed (the ball on the shelf). Jennifer helps Mommy (Daddy). Thank you, Jennifer." When you make this much fuss over her deed, she works to get more of this grand attention.

Your child learns from firsthand experiences—from exploring and discovering, from trial and error, from repetition, from practicing (which you allow). But she learns most through relationships (which you determine):

● When you provide materials for learning,
● When you patiently resist helping him until he asks,
● When you give him the help he asks for but no more,
● When you let him do for himself what he can do,
● When you show him how when he finds a task too difficult,

- When you put into words what he is doing and has done,
- When you encourage him with words, claps, and affection,
  —you champion his efforts to succeed;
  —he learns he is a person of value and worth;
  —he learns he is able and capable;
  —he attempts with eagerness his next task.

To him, learning is a joyful discovery.

What Your Child Can Learn About God

If your child gets her first notions about what God is like from what her parents are like, this is your grand opportunity to show your child that God is patient. God is patient with us when we stumble, get into things we should not, want to do everything our own way, and clutter things that we don't put back in their rightful place. When you have noticed how patient and lovingly God guides you, you will want your child to experience that same God.

This period from the time your child learns to walk until about eighteen months marks a turning point in your child's development as well as the way you relate to your child. How you respond to your child's budding independence and persistence to do it herself will affect her mental health and feelings of adequacy. Your treatment of her will influence whether she will have social or mental problems.

During this time, the child must assert her will to develop as a person in her own right. Sometimes this challenge of wills is viewed as misbehavior. Misbehavior is in the eye of the beholder. If you break a child's will, you break a child's spirit. As the patient parent and authority over this small child, you will take into account (1) the need to explore (without an awareness of danger or property value or rights), (2) the growing ability to understand words (with little ability to adequately express herself), and (3) the need to become a person with her own identity and independence.

If you think you are having a problem with your child who is awkward, curious, and striving for control and independence from you, just think what your child is going through. She has so much work to do and so little awareness of danger or of the trouble she can get into.

You will have many opportunities to comfort and soothe her hurts and frustrations. As you hold your child close to you and speak comforting words when she is afraid or hurt, she gets her first human feelings of solace on which to base her later understanding of God's comfort. As parents care for their suffering child, even so your Heavenly Father comforts you.

When your child is gaining control and has so little control, he needs the security of knowing you are in control. He has a quick temper which is easily aroused and loudly expressed. He expresses strong emotions, frustrations, hopelessness, despair, preferences. This is his way to communicate his feelings to you and to let you know his uniquenesses.

McIntyre was strapped in his car seat in the back of his mother's car but not without screaming resistance. Sitting alongside him was his grandmother whom they were driving to the airport. Grandmother leaned over and whispered (that got his attention momentarily) in his ear, "Grandmother is not afraid of your crying." McIntyre looked as if he thought, *That lady knows what she is talking about. She feels safe and secure, and so can I.* McIntyre was easily distracted as they passed a big eighteen-wheeler. "Truck." Grandmother said, "Look at the big truck!" McIntyre looked out the window with eagerness and said, "Truck, b-i-i-i-g truck."

When your child's accident causes a scratch and some bleeding, you can wash the wound with soap and water and kiss it (near it) to make it well. This old expression works. Mind over matter or body and healthy, nourished emotions over pain really work. Knowing that healing is within the body, you can genuinely say to the child, "God will help it get better (well)."

Your child gets his basic understanding of what God is like from the way you treat him.

You want your child to grow as God made him able to grow. He must first develop independence, a feeling of separateness from others and the ability to do for himself. You will help him develop feelings of his own personhood and worth as you allow him to learn with enthusiasm, call him by name when he tries or practices emerging skills, and when you show him your satisfaction with his efforts toward success. God wants each person to know he is valuable and worthwhile, that he is special to God.

You are the one who gives your child his first feelings of family. These basic attitudes help lay the foundation for his adult concept of earthly family and family of God. As you show your child pictures of Jesus at different ages, he is ready to hear that: Jesus had a family. His mother loved Him. Jesus went to church. Jesus loves you. Your child will think of Jesus as a person most like you.

Happy experiences at church help your child associate church with happy times with people who love and care for him. This lays the basic foundation for experiencing and learning that the church is a fellowship. When your child says, "Go church," expressing to you his desire to go to church, you know that he has happy times in his room with people who make him feel valuable and worthwhile. How important it is for little children to see both men and women in their departments!

Hopefully, every time your child goes to church, he has an opportunity to handle the Bible, to see pictures of Jesus and things God made, to hear songs, to work puzzles, to listen to recordings, to care for the baby (doll), to pretend to do those things he sees Mother and Daddy doing to help at home, to read books, and to build with blocks. All of these activities provide the child with natural situations in which teachers can talk about God and His love for your child.

As he explores things God made with his senses (eyes, nose, mouth, hands), he can hear you say that God gave him eyes to see (a nose to smell, and a tongue to taste) the banana. He will need to hear you say "God made the banana for Ashley to eat" many times before he will learn the concept of what God made.

How to Guide Your Child Toward God

Yours is the glorious privilege of introducing your child to God. You are instructed to bring up your child in "the nurture and admonition of the Lord" (Eph. 6:4). To nurture means to provide an atmosphere conducive to learning. Admonition has to do with instruction, teaching. Both nurture and admonition are needed. You can provide the environment which assists your child in learning those skills and developing those body functions which are crucial to this age and stage. Provide many opportunities for your child to hear, "God made you," "God made you to grow," "God gave you feet (for walking)," "God gave you eyes (to see the dog)."

When Jonathan is doing something to help (even if it is pretend), this is the time to say, "Thank you, Jonathan, for washing the dishes (handing Mother the dish)."

Give LeAnn choices within reason so she can learn to make choices. "You can read *this* book or *this* book. Which do you choose?" LeAnn begins to feel like a person with rights. She has a choice. Then she feels responsible for the choice she makes.

The family is God's design for nurturing young children and bringing them up in His ways. Guide Brent in his understanding of family. Use the word often to help him get an idea of its meaning. Say: "God gave Brent a mother. God gave Brent a daddy. Mother and Daddy love Brent."

As you drive to church, say, "Brent and Mother and Daddy drive to church in the car." Or, when Daddy is helping Brent put on his clothes, Mother can say, "Daddy is helping Brent put on his clothes. Daddy loves Brent."

Before bedtime when the family is together for reading the Bible and praying, Shelley can sit on Daddy's lap and turn the pages or open the Bible to the red ribbon. The three can sing a song such as "Jesus Loves Me."

Your child likes to be with the family so much that you can expect her to delay bedtime. A time of togetherness and warm feelings of love just before sleep gives a child the best preparation for healthy, restful sleep.

Remember the Bible verse quoted at the beginning of this chapter? It begins, "Parents, do not treat your children in such a way to make them angry." This verse needs to be constantly in the mind and heart of the parent of a toddler. That is because your child will appear to be exasperating and naughty at times. You will know that your child is not deliberately trying to annoy you. He is so limited in his understanding of what he should and should not do. His body and mind are in constant motion moved by a God-given curiosity which is vital to learning.

When your child drops the spoon from her high-chair tray, you pick it up. She drops it again and each time you pick it up. She is not trying to upset you. Remember when she was tiny and her little hand touched your hair and she got a handful in a locked grip. She was using her grasp reflex. Now she has discovered that she can release an object in her hand. She is practicing her newly discovered skill. Also, she is learning cause and effect. She drops (cause), you pick it up (effect). To her, she has discovered how to play the "I-drop-it, you-pick-it-up" game. Enjoy your child's learning activity.

If you shame Carole for dropping her spoon, you will cause her to doubt her body's wisdom to learn. She was not being naughty. Show your pleasure over her attainment. God is good to make her able to grow and learn new things.

David in his attempts to love Rhonda, who is about a year old, may bite instead of kiss. He is as surprised as the screaming victim at the result. He has not yet learned cause and effect. He has seen others put their mouths against a face. He wants to do this, too. He does not feel the pain. What he did felt good to him. David's intent was to kiss, not hurt. Remove him or remove the baby from his reach. David will need to be carefully supervised when he is close to the baby. Distract him by showing him a toy.

Dayne may dump the wastebasket (that is what he has seen you do), but where he dumps it will be a different place. Give him a wastebasket of his own with old mail (letters and magazines) which it is all right to dump. You have provided an environment for learning.

This is the time when your child will be noticing everything you do and will be trying to do what you do and be like you. What example do you want to give? She will be "dusting" the furniture, "talking" on the telephone (listen, and you will hear her say what she has heard you say), "cooking" in the kitchen. While your child enjoys imitating (to the child it is for real), she also enjoys helping you. Capitalize on each opportunity when your child wants to help. Give the child something to do which she can do safely and successfully. She can grow up feeling helpful and responsible. You are encouraging her God-given need to be on her own and to help other people.

She does not always obey. She is not being naughty. She has to learn what instructions mean. You can help her do what you have asked her to do. If you ask her to move to another spot, you may need to pick her up and put her in a safe place. As you are gentle and kind to her, she will best learn the meaning of the Bible thought, "Be kind to one another" (Eph. 4:32).

Expect little sharing during this time. Your child is just now learning "me" and "mine." He may still call himself Don because that is what you call him. Just keep noticing every occasion when he gives up a toy for a while. Sharing requires seeing from another's point of view. Your child is just now learning how he feels about what he possesses. What he possesses, he owns. Be patient with where he is in his understanding.

You guide your child toward God, his Creator, who made him able to become a unique person when you:

● are an example of patient love and encouragement as he practices his new skills of walking and doing for himself,

● tell him during affectionate moments that you love him, God loves him, and Jesus loves him,

● help him discover the awe and wonder of the things God made and say thank you to God for these, and

● "read" the Bible together as he shows interest.

Then Jesus called the children over to him and said to the disciples, "Let the little children come to me! Never send them away! For the Kingdom of God belongs to men who have hearts as trusting as these little children's. And anyone who doesn't have their kind of faith will never get within the Kingdom's gates" (Luke 18:16-17, TLB).

4
The Third Year: Gaining Self-Control

Your two-year-old is like the toddler, except more so. The major task continues to be gaining a sense of control over his body so that he can do things for himself—be independent. Heretofore known as the "terrible twos," let's start thinking of them as the "terrific twos."

What to Expect of Your Child

A remarkable change occurs in your child's thinking with his growing ability to understand and use language. His new ability to represent experience (to remember it later) puts him at a higher level of thinking. Before, it required actual contact with an object or person to think about either. Now he can think with the mental images he has stored in his mind. Before two years of age, he understood much more than he could say. His two-word sentences now expand to complete sentences. Instead of "Caught fish," he says, "I caught a fish at Big Daddy's." Notice that he says "I," whereas he used to say "Randy." Because your child's vocabulary may mount to almost a thousand words during this year, you may be tempted to expect too much of his behavior. His thinking is very limited. Remember, your child is a great imitator. A two-year-old entered his Aunt Lou's house and greeted her with a hug and blurted out, "I wuv you very much."

Notice that the child could pronounce most of the vowel sounds but may have trouble with some of the consonants. Be a good example of clear speech, and your child will learn to correct himself. Please omit formal lessons in grammar.

His use of language will help him organize his world and will give him better control over his behavior. Here is how it works. He can organize his world on the basis of time information. When Mother says, "Wait a minute," he knows that she will be available in a short while. He can wait. As Mother and Daddy talk about yesterday, the child puts activities into perspective. "Yesterday we went to church. Today we play at home. Tomorrow we go to Grandmother's house." He sees how he fits into the picture. As Mother uses numbers and the words *more* or *less*, he gets some concept of quantity and limits.

At the grocery store as Mother and Daniel are checking out, Daniel picks up a piece of candy, a package of gum, and a balloon. Mother noticed the three items. "Daniel, I said that you could have one package of gum or one balloon. Which do you choose?" Daniel put the balloon and candy back where he got them. "You chose the gum. Mother will pay for the gum." Before Mother could finish paying the bill, she noticed Daniel walking down the grocery aisle. This was unlike him. Before she got upset, she went for him. He was just turning the corner and was putting his gum wrapper into a wastebasket which he had spotted earlier. She was glad she had not reprimanded him. She said, "You wanted to put your gum wrapper in the wastebasket. Thank you, Daniel."

Alma is getting an understanding of classification—that is that things alike go together. She is learning, as did Daniel, that things have places. So she learns that knives go in one space, spoons in another. She can help put the silverware away. She learns that blocks go on one shelf, books on another, and toys on another. She learns to put up what she uses. This sense of organization about her world gives her a sense of security. She enjoys the routine which she has established, and she does not want it interrupted.

Bedtime is not a child's favorite time because she is now aware that the fun stops for her but the rest of the family gets to keep on having fun. Help your child establish a happy, bedtime ritual which involves all the family. Let bathtime be not just for cleaning but for pleasure. Supply your child with bathtub toys, bubble bath, and let her play (you will have to anticipate your own schedule to plan for this). What you have discovered is that she has a long attention span when she is absorbed in what she wants to do. After bath is storytime. She gets to snuggle on a parent's lap and "read" the Bible before going to bed. Go to the child's room and spend some unrushed, quality time holding your child close to you, telling her you love her, kissing her, and smiling as you tuck her into bed. Read her a book or a story of her choice. Going to bed can be a pleasant experience for your child.

Your child knows what he likes to eat and can name it. Mother knew that Josh had been to a pizza party for birthday dinner and that he probably would not want much for the evening meal. She could trust his body wisdom because at home she only gave him nutritious food. Mack responded quickly, "Bread and rice." So he had brown bread and brown rice for dinner.

Your child will enjoy using the phone now that she can talk in words and sentences rather than jargon and jibberish. When Grandmother called Jennifer's house, a friend who was keeping Jennifer answered the phone. When Jennifer came to the phone, Grandmother asked, "Where are Mother and Daddy?" Jennifer could answer, "Gone to Bible study." She does not know what Bible study is, but her parents are careful to tell her where they are going and when they will return.

She is now learning to use her hands and feet. She can now do fairly well at dressing herself, brushing her teeth, washing her face, and using the toilet. Being able to do for herself gives her confidence in her abilities.

The toys she used as a toddler are still enjoyable, but she uses them in more complex ways. Hands are adept to turn knobs, insert keys, turn crank handles, draw, paint, use cutters with play dough, set the table, and stir the eggs (help with cooking). Feet are ready to climb the ladder, turn the pedals on a tricycle, and climb stairs.

During the last three months of this year, just before she is three, accept her need to feel like a baby again. Give the wanted attention, and she will soon be behaving like a three-year-old.

What Your Child Needs

This period marks a transition from babyhood to childhood. Growing up is difficult, especially for a two-year-old. His life is filled with stress. If he does not achieve a marked degree of independence and feelings of confidence and competence during this year, these will be more difficult to attain each year thereafter. You do not want your child as a grown-up to feel dependent on you or others. This kind of dependency later on causes a person to be vulnerable to cults whose leaders will do their thinking for them.

Now that he has a will of his own and knows that he has choices, he has to make some major decisions with his limited maturity. When should he stop doing what he wants to do when you ask him to? When should he do what you want him to do when he doesn't want to? Should he always conform, or should he sometimes get to do it "my way"? Big decisions! This is also the time his conscience is developing. He is getting a beginning idea of what is right to do and wrong to do. The behaviors you stop, he learns are wrong; the behaviors you allow, he learns are right. Be sure that the behaviors you stop are really wrong, or you may have a child with an overdeveloped conscience. If you stop him from walking on the grass, he may learn never to walk on the grass. He would be denied an exhilarating experience, especially barefooted. On the other hand, the behaviors you condone should be really right lest he continue doing something which is not so "cute" later.

If you want your child to become a person who can think for himself, help him feel confident about what he can do. Feel competent yourself, then you will feel better able to give him reasonable choices. Notice his efforts to conform to socially acceptable behavior. Be patient when he is attempting an impossible task. Be nearby to tell him how he feels so he can understand his strange emotions. Understand his limited ability to share his mother and daddy and toys.

When a child is three, he will be better able to have a measure of independence and more easily accept a new baby in his home. At times he may still feel somewhat left out unless you plan to spend special times just with him. Matthew's baby brother seemed to be getting more attention than he, so he climbed onto Mother's lap, nestled down like a baby, and started making baby sounds. Mother, knowing his need, held him lovingly, rocked him gently, and talked to him soothingly until he felt loved and secure. To shame your child for acting as a baby or to try to convince him of how big he is will not give him the attention he is begging for.

When your child feels that the new baby is an intruder and he would really like to swat her, you can say: "You feel angry with Jessica. You think Mother and Daddy love her more than they love you." You will notice that he feels comfort in hearing you express what he cannot. To try to convince a child that he loves his sister will only confuse him.

Your child needs your patience and understanding with toilet training. Take a relaxed view. You cannot train a child until his body muscles are ready, and the child is willing. If you have a warm, loving relationship with your child, he will enjoy your pleasure over his successes. He wants to feel big and to please you. If you put pressure on him when he is not ready, he will feel inadequate, incompetent, and frustrated. Learning to restrain the flow of urine and the movement of the bowels is a difficult task. Heretofore, these movements occurred naturally without any help from him. When you see him touching his pants or turning red in the face, you may say, "I believe you need to go to the toilet." Recognize his efforts to succeed, accept the "accidents," change him, and assure him of your love.

Your child has mixed emotions at this time. She tries the impossible, resists your help, and cries when you won't help. She wants, and she doesn't want. At other times, she wants you to dress her just like you dress the baby. Because she is at extremes, she needs you to be flexible. Consistently, accept her feelings, stop her destructive or hurtful or annoying behavior, assure her of your love, cheer her on when she is behaving appropriately, and wait until about age three for definite rules and limits. You will help her develop a stable sense of personhood.

When you make too many demands to control her and make her conform, she becomes more dependent and submissive. She may appear to be obedient and quiet, even "nice." She may grow up to be a shy adult, afraid to think for herself and to try new things. On the other hand, an overcontrolled child may never give in to her parents' demands and go through life with a chip on her shoulder always feeling the need to fight battles that may not be there. Another child may outwardly conform but harbor resentment ready to lash out at whatever she can. Or the person may grow up thinking she is righteous when filled with resentment.

The other caution is that of under control—allowing the child to do anything without regard for the rights of others. Anytime a child is hurting himself or abusing the rights of others, he should be stopped. A child needs to feel safe and secure. He feels safe when he knows his mother or father is in control and will not let him hurt himself or another nor let him destroy property. How you respond to your child's needs during this crucial stage when he learns who he is, will largely determine how he will feel about himself and relate to others as an adult. Nurture in him the calmness and assurance of your faith and your ability to be in control when he is out of control. Let him know that he can trust you to keep him from hurting or annoying others. Let him know that you love him no matter what happens (unconditional love).

What Your Child Can Learn About God

God is redemptive. He wants the best for us. Even when we are unlovely and unlovable, He loves us still. God may abhor what we do, but He loves us. He wants to forgive and reclaim us. Your two-year-old will present you with numerous opportunities to love him when he has been unloving and out of control. How you relate to your child during these trying moments will give him his first views of what God is like—how God relates to people—to him.

What you think about God largely determines what you think about yourself. If you believe God is loving and kind and is "not willing that any should perish" (2 Pet. 3:9), then you can find comfort in what Jesus did in life and death to ensure our hope of life eternal with God and fullness of life with Him here. You may realize your own worth and value before God. When you feel valuable and worthwhile, you can best assist your child in feeling that way.

Your child is growing in his concept of God as he grows in his understanding of you. Later when he hears the parent term, *Father,* by which God is called, he has warm thoughts, feelings, and associations because the word *father* stirs up loving feelings.

Thus, a child learns that God is a person and in his small mind, most like the important people in his life because that is all he has to associate with persons.

You can help lay foundations for his understanding that God made people. This concept will take time. He can learn to value people as you say, "God made people," "God made me," "God made Daddy," "God made you." He will accept what you say although he does not fully understand.

When you say to her, "God loves you," as you hold her in a tender embrace, she feels your arms and your love. She also is getting thoughts that someone else loves her. As you mention, "God loves Sara, and God loves John," your child learns that God loves people.

You want your child to know that God wants people to love Him. One of the ways you can show your love for God which will be an example to your child is to say thank you to God for the things He has given you. "Thank You, God, for giving us Leslie. We love her very much."

Give your child a sense of awe and wonder at the things God

made. Observe the robin hopping about on the lawn pulling worms from the ground. "Look, Rachel, see the bird! God made the bird. The bird found a worm to eat. God made the worm for the bird to eat."

At Christmas you can talk about the baby Jesus. Talk about how His mother loved Him and how Joseph loved Him. Show a picture in the Bible of Jesus as a baby to your child. He can sense that Jesus grew. "He got bigger and bigger like you. Jesus helped His mother. Maybe He brought the water to her." Your child will associate Jesus with the Bible and will get the feeling that Jesus is important to you.

The child's concept of Jesus includes a growing understanding of: Jesus grew to be a boy, then a man. Jesus had a family. Jesus helped His family. Jesus loves him. Jesus loves people. Jesus wants people to love and help each other.

Foundations are laid to help the child feel he is important to God and to other persons. Anytime someone is showing loving care and respect to your child, you can say: "Mrs. Bridges loves you. She brought you some bananas." "Mr. Hargrove loves you. He came to play with you."

Your child can become increasingly aware that God made him special. He can learn that he is a person of value who deserves respect. He can learn to control his emotions if you accept his feelings. You need, however, in a loving way to stop his actions which do not respect the rights of others, such as hitting, pushing, shoving, biting, spitting, throwing things, destroying property, or annoying. Too many restrictions are unreasonable.

How to Guide Your Child Toward God

Throughout the day and night whenever you are showing love to your child tell Jena that you love her, and God loves her, too. She learns that love is a kiss, a hug, a smile, a warm pat, a wink of approval or recognition, and kind words.

As Robert spreads the salad dressing on the buns, Mother (Daddy) can say, "Thank you, Robert, for helping make the hamburgers. God is good to give us hands so we can help." When your child hears that God made his hands to help, he is growing in his concept of God's love and goodness.

At the lunch table, Robert hears you pray: "Thank You, God, for Robert. Robert is growing. Robert likes to help. We are so glad you gave him to us. Thank You, God, for the food, for the lettuce, the tomato, the hamburger meat, and the milk. Amen." Robert learns that you can talk to God. He learns that the people in families help each other. As he is helped, he wants to help others in his family.

Notice attempts your child makes at playing house. This is her way to understand how family members help at home. Your child will pretend to feed the baby, cook a meal, or dust the furniture. She imitates what she sees you or others doing. Help her become an important member of the family by allowing her to help. Thank her for helping even when she is pretending. What she is doing is real to her. "Thank you for feeding your baby. You are helping the baby. The Bible tells us to help each other."

Through playing with other children, your child gains a growing understanding of the views of others. Twos want to "do it my way." The ways they want to do things are different. Another child learns that Katy likes to paint, but he likes to build with blocks. Your child learns from you how you view things. She is very sensitive to your feelings, your moods, and emotions. Missy has just accidentally knocked over a glass of milk. Mother's expression spoke louder than her words. Seeing the tired and frustrated look on Mother's face, Missy walked over to her, patted her, and said, "I'm sorry." Missy was not afraid of her mother. She had spilled milk before and heard her mother say, "You spilled your milk. You didn't mean to. Mother will help you clean it up."

As you pray, you may want to hold Robert's hands. He feels your touch during quiet and thankful moments and feels more a part of the family.

You cannot take your child to Jesus and have Jesus hold him lovingly, talk to him, and pray with him. You can "let your child come to Jesus" by introducing him to Jesus.

Opening your Bible to a picture of Jesus and the children, sing, or say: "I open my Bible, and what do I see? A picture of Jesus, He loves Jess and me" (*Songs for the Young Child,* Bill Leach, Broadman). Touch the picture of Jesus, and say: "This is a picture of Jesus. Jesus loves this boy (girl). (Touch the picture of a child.) Jesus loves you, Jess." When the child has happy experiences holding the Bible, seeing the pictures, turning the pages, and hearing its stories, he wants to have other experiences with it.

Every experience with Mother and Daddy and other members of the family give your child feelings and information about what a family is. Hearing her mother say "I'm glad God gave you to us" gives her a beginning understanding that God made families.

As a child is respected, he learns to respect others. Mark's father worked at night. During the day, he slept. Mark was learning to stay quiet, so Daddy could sleep. His Mother had just given him an old typewriter to use as a toy, a textbook for learning. Mark was learning to be considerate of others. During the day when Father was asleep, Mark asked, "Can I type?" He meant, "Will it be all right to type with Daddy sleeping?" His mother said, "Yes, just close the door to your room quietly."

Consideration for others grows out of self-respect and knowing that others are valuable and important.

This is a crucial period in social development, in getting along with other people. The patterns of social relationships are so well established by age three that they will be difficult to change. If you let your child have her way because of a temper tantrum or give in to her unreasonable demands, she will grow up knowing how to manipulate people and do whatever she needs to get her way. If you show respect to your child, meet her needs, and respect others, she, too, will learn that she has rights, and others have rights.

Every response to your child's behavior teaches her what God is like—not because God is like you but because her first thought about God is that God is a person most like her parents, the persons she knows most about. How you treat her teaches her what she is. Treat her as a gift of God. Celebrate her growing independence!

So Jesus called a child, had him stand in front of them, and said, "I assure you that unless you change and become like children, you will never enter the Kingdom of heaven" (Matt. 18:3, GNB).

5
The Fourth Year: Showing Concern for Others

Your difficult two-year-old becomes a delightful three-year-old. Walking and talking, learning to do for herself, becoming a person in her own right are difficult tasks for such a short period of time. From total dependency to one who has much self-control, your child can let you know her needs with words. She can get along with other people fairly well which shows remarkable progress.

What to Expect of Your Child

Now that your child is three, if you have given her freedom within limits to do for herself and have acclaimed all her attempts to do for herself, she is well on her way to cooperative behavior. She feels comfortable doing jobs which you tell her are helpful. She feels so big. She wants to be like you, do the things you do, and feel able and capable. She trusts you to treat her with kindness and respect. She learns that she is valuable and worthwhile. Now she is ready to play with other children. She may still play alongside another child without playing together even though they are playing with the same materials. As the year goes by you will notice that your child can play with another and can cooperate in playing house—taking care of the baby (doll).

She is still very self-centered, that is, seeing from only one point of view—hers. Before she can see from another's point of view, she has to know hers first. Playing with other children gives your child an opportunity to give and take, to take turns, to know what she can do and not do with others. As you guide her lovingly, she learns that she has rights and others have rights. At three, she notices the facial expressions of others and can distinguish between sad and happy, pleasure and displeasure, anger and satisfaction by looking at your face or hearing your voice.

Expect a lot of charm. She can smile to win you over and show warm affection generously. Enjoy all these expressive behaviors which she has learned by your example or your approval. The more you give, the more she will give. The more she feels loved and accepted, the more she will be able to love and accept others.

Your child may make unreasonable demands. He may scream to get his way. When you are in the grocery store and he makes a scene to get the cereal with the toy in the box, remember that he feels secure knowing what he can and cannot do. He feels secure knowing that you are decisive and know how to handle a situation. Be firm, gentle, and consistent. Soon he will feel good and know that *no* means *no* and he does not need to have a tantrum anymore; it just doesn't work.

This is a year of rapid brain growth. You will be aware of this as you notice how well your child can talk about most anything he needs, sees, and wants. He discovers his own rules for language. If he says, "She played the piano," he may say, "She throwed the ball." If you correct his grammar, he may be hesitant to speak. Let him express himself freely.

Mental growth develops quickly as the child has opportunity to work with blocks, puzzles, nature materials, housekeeping toys, books, pictures, and musical instruments and recordings. As he plays, you can observe what he is doing with the materials, put into words what he is doing, and talk with him. This is your way to know what your child needs to know and what is important to him. God wants his mind to develop toward its potential.

Your child is learning how to think. Even though time is abstract, she is gaining more understanding of what "wait a minute," tomorrow, today, and yesterday mean. She can talk about the weather and what she should wear. Numbers are becoming important. She can bring *one* book to you. She can match a piece of real fruit with a picture of the fruit.

As a toddler or a two-year-old, he sometimes said *no* when he meant *yes.* At three, he knows the meaning of *no.* He may say, "No, she not." You can talk back saying the words correctly, "No, she doesn't." You do not want him to think you are correcting him. You want him to know you have listened to him and heard what he said.

Value your child's questions. She will be asking, "What's that?" "Why?" "Where?" "When?" Answer as courteously as you would answer a friend. Encourage her curiosity and need to know. Each question presents a teachable moment.

He is now learning that he is a boy. He notices that Katy has on fingernail polish. He wants his nails polished. Mother says, "Girls wear fingernail polish." Then Grandmother comes. She puts fingernail polish on Mark. (Grandmothers do some things that mothers don't do. The child learns that Grandmother lets me do this, Mother doesn't.) When Mark proudly displayed his painted fingernails, he exclaimed, "Like Katy's!"

Your child is learning to be responsible. She can take some

responsibility for the materials she uses. She can remember simple routines. She recognizes that some things belong to Daddy, some to Mother, and some to other children. She knows something about "taking turns."

Your child is growing morally and spiritually. He can repeat things he hears about God and Jesus and remember short Bible stories and songs. He can pray short thank-you prayers.

Such dramatic changes occur as your child is able to become more thoughtful to others, take turns, and give and receive affection. However, he needs help in coping with his feelings.

What Your Child Needs

Your child's most important need is to feel loved. Of course your child's basic physical needs must be met, such as food, comfort, and activity. These, however, cannot sustain a child. The highest of God's creation, the human being, thrives on love. A child who feels loved is in the best position to show love and thoughtfulness and consideration. So much has been said about giving a child quality time that a recent cartoon showed a mother leaving her friends at the car, saying, "I must go in now and give my child a few seconds of quality time." Quality time takes time. Love needs to be shown in unhurried times when the child can absorb the feelings.

Feeling safe is a need which when met frees a child to use his energy in productive ways. He feels safe when he knows what he can and cannot do, and when you are consistent in your expectations. If you laugh among relatives when your child comes out with his first "four-letter-word" and reprimand him when he says it before his Sunday School teacher or the pastor, your child feels confused, unsafe.

Every child needs to feel that she belongs. Feeling a part of a family gives a child this sense of "I belong to my family, to my

Mother, and to my Daddy." Your three-year-old may feel very possessive of her parents when other children bid for their time. Kristin was on a camping trip with her parents and three other families. Older children were getting the attention of Kristin's daddy. She needed to stay near him. At home the next night, Kristin got in bed with Daddy and patted him while saying, "*My* Daddy. *My* Daddy."

Your child can feel that he belongs when the activities at church are at his level of understanding. How important that your child be able to learn Bible truths in natural situations so that he knows that the Bible is about life and how God wants us to live with others.

Feeling accepted for what she is encourages your child to keep on becoming the unique person which God designed. A child feels defeated when parents' expectations are not realistic. Anticipate and allow enough time for a child to do what you have asked. Learning under pressure creates worry. Three-year-olds need to feel unrushed so they can practice the numerous skills they need to learn this year.

Thoughtfulness toward others is best learned by example. As you accept your child's efforts, she learns to be thoughtful and tolerant of others. Melissa accidentally spilled her soup at the table. See this accident from her point of view. She probably feels most uncomfortable making such a mess. If you scold her for an accident, she may become fearful of her own abilities and fearful of others and how they respond when she messes up. She will stop risking opportunities to learn. She will shy away from people. How do you feel when you knock over a glass of tea? How do you want the other person to respond to you? Think through your own feelings in situations when you are with those who are older or superior to you, and you mess up. Then consciously remember the thought in Matthew 7:12—as you would want to be treated, treat your child in the same way. You will hear yourself saying: "That's all right, Melissa. You didn't mean to spill it. I will get two sponges, and we will clean it up." Fortunate is the child who has parents who understand their child's needs and are as thoughtful and considerate to their children as they are to their friends.

Your child needs to know that you understand his behavior. He does not know why he acts like he does. One frequent question asked is, "What do you do when your child and another friend the same age are playing together in the presence of their parents, and one grabs a toy from the other?" Why not turn your head? That method may shock you, but surely you want each child to learn to solve his own problems. If a parent begins serving as referee, the child learns that Mother or Daddy will solve his problem. The child whose toy was snatched will do something (scream, grab the toy, hit). Let children handle their own problems if you can bear to let them. Intervene when safety is a problem. Each child can profit from hearing you put into words what is happening. "Justin, you took the truck out of Adam's hands. Adam is crying. That is his way of telling you he doesn't like it. He wants the truck back." Then wait for Justin to think what he should do, then respond. Or say to Adam: "You don't like it because Justin took your truck. You can tell him you don't like it. You can ask him to give it back." The last resort would be to tell Justin to give the truck to Adam which you feel would solve the problem. What would Justin have learned? What would Adam have learned? Parents only see part of an ongoing activity. Adam may have taken it away from Justin before the parents got into the act.

If you want Justin to share, you will be courteous and ask him if he wants to. He may choose not to. You might say: "You have a choice. You can put your truck in your room and come back and play with Adam. Or you can play by yourself in your room with the truck."

Courtesy is consulting with a child. Do you want someone to tell you what you have to share? Respecting a child's decision will help him become more open with his true desires. If you force a child to give up his toy, you only increase his possession to keep it.

What Your Child Can Learn About God

During this year, your child will have a mental image of God as a person. He will accept what you say about God although what you say will not have the same meaning for the child as it does for you. You can say to him: "God made people. God made you. God made Mother. God made Daddy." If you are expecting another child, toward the end of your pregnancy you can tell your child that God is going to give you another baby.

During this time of learning consideration and kindness for others, you can say: "God made people to love and help each other. God made you, and God made Mommy. You are helping Mommy when you water the plants." "God made Nathan. Nathan is your friend. God loves Nathan. Matt loves Nathan."

Your child can learn that God made the earth. He made the ground for us to walk on. God made the green grass that tickles our bare feet. God made the blue, blue sky. God made the clouds. As a child experiences what God made, she may feel a sense of wonder when she sees things God made and hears about them. A child at three has difficulty distinguishing between what God made and what people made. When you dig in the dirt, plant a seed, and water it, the child may think that you caused the plant to grow. She can associate God with the things God made. A child learns through senses—what she sees, feels, hears, tastes, smells. God cannot be seen or touched, but the things God made can be experienced through the senses.

Your child can learn that the Bible tells about Jesus. She learns that Jesus is special. Jesus was born and grew to be a boy. He had a family. Mary was His mother, and Joseph was the father in the family. A child of three can hear you say that Jesus is God's Son, but she does not know what that means. To her the daddy is a man who lives with a child. She hears a story about Mary and Joseph and the baby Jesus, about Mary and Joseph taking the baby to church.

We use the word *church* instead of temple and synagogue, for he hears and experiences *church.* The child is just learning to use the word *church.* Later, he can learn the meaning of the other words. The child is learning that church is more than a place. Church is people. When you say, "Let's go to church," he is thinking of his friends and teachers and what they do together. When your child goes to his room at church, he should be learning: People at church talk and sing about God and Jesus. We read the Bible at church. We work and play together at church. My teachers at church love me. I have friends at church. I can help at church.

Your child can learn that Jesus loves him, and Jesus loves people. Jesus wants people to love and help each other. Jesus becomes an important person in the child's mind when Jesus is important to the significant people in a child's life, his parents and teachers.

Your child can hear that God made families. He wanted babies to have a mother and a daddy to care for and to love them. She can learn that she has a family. She has a mother, a daddy, and a brother or sister. She can learn to help in her family and enjoy the help which family members give her. Mainly, she can

learn that her family loves God and they love and help each
other.

At three, your child can understand that the Bible is a special
book. If she sees it only at church, she learns that it is a special
book to use at church. If she also sees it and uses it at home, she
learns that the Bible is a special book in her home. Plan for
happy experiences with the Bible at home. Your child can enjoy
hearing short stories and seeing pictures about Jesus and other
Bible characters. She can better understand when the stories
are about something to which she can relate. Miriam and her
baby brother (who was later named Moses), David and the
sheep, David and Jonathan, Timothy and his mother and grandmother are good examples. Tell the story only as the child shows
interest. Do not force the Bible on her or bombard her with it
day and night lest she learn to avoid an unpleasant experience.
Your goal is to have her want to know more and more about
what it says. She will be able to repeat the things she hears about
God and Jesus and remember brief stories, songs, and Bible
thoughts and verses. The child may associate warm thoughts
with using the Bible as she gets to sit in Daddy's or Mommy's
lap when they "read" it.

You are the authority over your child. He thinks you are
infallible, that you do not make mistakes. Whatever you tell the
child, he accepts without question. How important that we tell
the child what he can understand lest he distort the meaning!

The Bible teaches that each person is of worth and value to
God. The Bible is a love story of God for the people He made.
He wants the best for us. He wants each person to have fullness
of life, to become what God has made him able to become, to
be partakers of His goodness, and responsible to care for the
things He made. God loved us enough to send Jesus to show us
He loved us and how we should live. God wants you to help your

three-year-old know that he is important. God made him. God loves him. God made him able to help in special ways. When the child feels loved and valued, he is best able to be kind and considerate of others.

How to Guide Your Child Toward God

Above all, you can guide your child toward God by showing him godly love—the love which is patient and kind and not rude. No occasion warrants a parent being disrespectful of a child, his innocence, and his dependence on the authority over him. Some parents think they love their children, but the children don't know it. Some parents equate strict discipline with love. A parent may be strict in order to meet his own need for authority, to control somebody. Parental control should be done in love for the child's good. Some ways in which you can show love so your child will know it are:

(1) Look into your child's eyes frequently. Make eye contact as you greet your child, talk with your child, and love your child. Look into her eyes at a short distance with love. Use your eyes for love, not for punishment. If you use your eyes mainly for punishment, you may find that your child avoids looking into your eyes.

(2) Show your child physical affection in numerous and constant ways by touching, hugging, patting, kissing, putting your face next to his. Appropriate and courteous physical contact communicates care. Adults enjoy a friendly touch, also. Parents should show tender love and care to their own children. The children should see them showing loving care to all people. Love shown when a child is hurt, upset, or frightened can comfort, console, and restore. When your child has an accident on the tricycle or bumps his head under a table, hold him tenderly and say, "I'm sorry you are hurt." The love you give your child

will come back to you. Love multiplies. Love cannot be kept; it must be shared.

(3) When your child talks to you, show your interest by listening. This tells the child that what he thinks or needs is important to you. Say back to the child what she has said to you. "You can't find your car and you want me to help you find it." "You want to talk on the telephone."

(4) Teach your child (discipline) so that he knows what is helpful to do and what is hurtful. Comment frequently on your child's attempts to help with the jobs at home, to show kindness to his friends. Thank your child throughout the day for giving you a kiss, for feeding the dog, for letting a friend play with his toy, for brushing his teeth, for putting his toys away. Stop his destructive, annoying, and hurtful behaviors. Say firmly and lovingly: "I can't let you hit. It hurts Jason when you hit him. People are not for hitting. People are for loving." Giving a reason with every rule or restraint teaches the child why.

When the child hears you say, "God loves you, Carrie," Carrie can believe that God loves her because she has experienced that you love her. She has good feelings about this God whom she has never seen. She learns that she is important to the special people in her life, and God is important to her.

Your three-year-old is self-centered, but she can share if she has an example of sharing.

No day should pass without a child hearing God's name used in a respectable way. "God made you, Robin. God loves you. I thank God for giving you to us." Each day discover with your child some wonder which God has given. A frisky squirrel is leaping from one limb of a tree to another. "Look, Lynn, God made the squirrel so he could fly from one tree to another. God made the squirrel so he could find his food." "Thank You, God, for the bunny that hops around on the ground looking for food to eat."

When your child does something inappropriate, don't ask him why he did it. He doesn't know. Adults don't always know why they do things. Nor should you ask a child if he broke something or left his clothes on the floor. When you know the answer, don't set him up for lying. You can tell him in words how you feel. "You broke the glass, but you didn't mean to." "I'd like for you to pick up your clothes, then I won't stumble over them."

Bring God into the ordinary. In this way the child learns that he can be closely associated with God. How sad to hear of a grown man who said he was brought up in a Christian home with strict parents but never knew until he was an adult that he could have an intimate, personal relationship with God!

If you love someone, you talk about it and show it. Talk to your child throughout the day about God's love and how Jesus helped people. Use Bible stories, songs, and verses as your child is experiencing something with which she can associate the Bible truths. When your child is helping you take care of your baby may be a good time to say a few sentences about Miriam. "You help Mommy take care of Robert when you bring to me his diapers. There is a story in the Bible about Miriam. Miriam had a baby brother, too. She helped take care of her baby brother." Or Mother could have said, "In our Bible it says, 'Help one another.'" You are doing what God wants you to do. God wants you to help. You help Mother by bringing the diapers." Or Mother could have sung: "Sally is a helper. Sally is a helper. Sally brings me diapers. Sally is a helper." If you sing songs, your child will learn them and sing them. What a joy to hear your child singing or saying Bible truths at meaningful times! Also, when she remembers to say thank you to God for food or sings songs to her "baby," you feel grateful that your child is growing toward God.

A child learns about God mostly through relationships. When you have established a trust relationship with your child and your child feels loved, you have laid a solid foundation for guiding your child toward God.

*Love is very patient and kind, . . . never . . . selfish
or rude. . . . does not demand its own way. . . . is not
irritable or touchy* (1 Cor. 13:4-5, TLB). *Love
never gives up; and its faith, hope, and patience
never fail* (v. 7, GNB).

6
The Fifth Year:
Creating His Own Ideas

What to Expect of Your Child

Demanding, frustrating, out-of-bounds, loud, highly imaginative four-year-old! This is an even year when life is difficult for the child because of the changes in his body and increased expectations of parents. His body has been growing so rapidly that his coordination has not kept up. He now stumbles up the stairs when at three he could walk up them. When your child is frustrated—and he is much of the time—he hits, kicks, throws, breaks things, and runs away. And that is not all he does. He uses loud, silly laughter, has fits of rage, and says words that shock parents. He seems to enjoy defying adult demands. He tells tall tales because of his vivid imagination. To unknowing adults his imagination is unreasonable—not a very pleasant picture. God is good to give parents variety in what to expect of the child. The plan is easy to keep in mind: The even years are difficult (for the child and perhaps for parents), and the odd years are smooth and delightful.

During this year, your child will have difficulty getting along with an older brother or sister and will be rough and inconsiderate with a younger child. The result will be fighting and quarreling. She is so self-centered, unable to see from the point of view of the older or younger child that she strikes out at others to meet her own needs.

His experience is limited. When two children are playing with blocks, each may reach for the same block and tug to see who can get it from the other. Learning "what's mine" is a task for this year. To share, one must know that he owns, that something is his, and then he must give it up to another (without ever getting it back).

At times you will be quite exasperated because of the four-year-old's imagination. A desperate parent will say, "My child is lying. What should I do?"

Well, one of the main characteristics of a four-year-old is that she has problems separating reality and imagination, fact from fancy. What she imagines (sees in her head) is as real to her as can be. She has dreams, and her mind sees all sorts of unusual things. When she is awake at night, she may have dreams of similar things. Life is unstable for your child because of this stage of development and because we know least about what is happening to the child during this stage. We think she is one year older and should be acting older. Memory is a mental picture which a child has stored in her mind. When other mental pictures appear in her mind, she cannot sort them out in the two categories of real and make-believe. Both pictures appear in her mind. Whatever appears in her mind is real to her.

Adults can understand this characteristic because they play imaginary games with their child, such as the Tooth Fairy, Easter Bunny, and Santa Claus. A child without imagination would never enjoy such games. So your child is illogical. When you talk about an Easter bunny and eggs, he sees no problem with the fact that a bunny does not lay eggs and cannot carry them in his paws to hide them from boys and girls. To your four-year-old, the Tooth Fairy, Easter Bunny, Sandman, and Santa Claus are real. They are not make-believe. Your child depends on you to tell him what is right. He will not question because he is illogical and cannot separate real from make-believe. He makes judgments on what he sees, not on logic. Why are we so inconsistent in our expectations? On the one hand, we expect our child to be illogical and believe in imaginary creatures. On the other hand, we expect him to tell the truth and do not accept his grand imagination. If he tells you what he imagines, and he cannot separate what he thinks from what is real, is he lying?

At three and a half and even at four, your child when he is playing gets so engrossed in being a cat or Superman or Wonder Woman or R2D2 that he really *is* that thing or person for the time. Ask a four-year-old if Superman or R2D2 is real, and see what he says. Think how confusing for a four-year-old to separate fact and fiction as he watches television. Even adults have difficulty at times coping with the problem of what is real and what is make believe on television. A movie rendition of a potential nuclear disaster aired on TV caused great anxiety in adults who thought they were viewing the news.

Your child cannot think abstractly. She thinks literally. This means that she thinks from her own experiences and puts into words the meaning they have for her. If words have a deeper meaning than their first meaning, the child will get the first meaning. When your child sings, "This little light of mine," she thinks about the only kind of light she has experienced. The word *light* cannot stand for something other than light or light bulb.

A child was told that her uncle had open-heart surgery. She wanted to know if the doctor let Jesus out of his heart. You say to a child that Jesus is in your heart, and since she is illogical, she gets a mental picture of a little man in the part of the body which we call *heart*. She does not think of the abstract meaning that Jesus now provides the motivation for all our behaviors.

A four-year-old's grandmother died, and his father told him that Grandmother had gone to heaven. "Well, let's go see her, then." Heaven to the child is a place like the one where he lives. He cannot think of a spiritual place.

When your child expresses himself through such materials as paint, blocks, and homeliving toys, you will notice that he has ideas of his own. He uses the experience he has to put things together in different ways. He draws or paints pictures of things he thinks about. He tries to make them real. If Kevin has seen an electric train, he may draw a picture of a real train with a cord. When he plays with blocks, he may build one thing, then build several different things before he has finished. You will notice that he thinks about what he is going to build and usually follows through with it. With his active imagination, you may notice the unusual in his creations.

In his search for realism, your child will talk with you at length about all the details he has about a subject. If he has experienced a tornado warning or watch lately and you have read to him from a book about storms, he may show a keen interest in the subject. He wants to know all the details. At times he seems so grown up. You may even think of him as the "little philosopher." He feels so grown up when he can use words to express himself and you talk with him about the subject of interest, although he may understand little of it.

Toward the middle of this year, your child will be better able to cope with her frustration. She is gaining control of her hands and feet. With the ability to control her hands and feet, she can use pencils, crayons, and brushes to draw, paint, and write. Your child wants to write her name and draw letters and numbers.

Has your child ever wanted to know what her backside looked like? You may find a child drawing her face and turning the paper over to draw the back of the head.

She is interested in where babies come from. She may accept that a baby grows in the mother's abdomen. Since she is now most conscious of the navel, however, she may wonder if that's where the baby comes out.

What Your Child Needs

Perhaps more than ever before, your child needs to know that you love him even when you don't like the way he is behaving. Most of all, he needs unconditional love—love that does not depend on how well he behaves or performs. Your child will not feel fully loved until he knows that you are going to love him regardless of his behavior.

Every child needs parents who understand him, who understand what to expect at each stage of a child's development. Your child feels loved when he knows that you understand what being four years old is all about.

—Love is accepting his need to own things before he can share.

—Love is understanding that he can see only from his limited point of view.

—Love is knowing that sharing is difficult when a child is just learning what is his and what is Daddy's or Mother's or Sister's.

—Love is understanding that what he imagines is real to him.

—Love is responding to his out-of-bounds behavior with patience.

—Love is accepting his reality.

—Love is helping a child express his feelings with words instead of hitting, pushing, biting.

—Love notices a child's efforts to use his own ideas to think for himself.

—Love lets a child be a child. Love sees from his point of view and meets his childish needs.

—Love rejoices with the child when he experiences gladness and feels his pain when he is hurt.

—Love understands and ministers when the child is frustrated, upset, afraid, angry, and rebellious, knowing that the child can learn from the parent's considerate behavior and words.

Have you ever said to your child, "I don't know what I am going to do to you?" Had you ever thought how this makes your child feel? He thinks you know everything, at least everything you need to know to answer his questions and take care of his needs. During this year when he hardly knows what to do with himself and a whole range of uncomfortable feelings, he needs to know that you can handle whatever comes your way. He feels secure when he trusts that he can depend on you to control him when he is out of control. If you don't know and he doesn't know, just think how unsafe and insecure he must feel.

He feels secure when he knows you understand how he feels —when you put into words what he is feeling. You can help him deal positively with his feelings so that he does not have to resort to hurtful, destructive acts. You can give your child words to use to talk about how he feels. Sometimes that is enough to reduce the anger and the need to strike out. You might say: "Tell Scott you don't like it when he takes your blocks." "You are upset because you can't go outside now." "You are afraid of the loud noise." "You are sleepy, but you don't want to go to bed."

Your child will learn from your example. When Karen and Mother went to the park to watch the ducks, one duck was floating with its head down. Karen asked, "What happened?"

"The duck is dead. It can't lift its head," said Mother.

"That's sad," responded Karen. She is learning to express feelings.

A child has feelings. She cannot help her feelings. She can gain control of destructive behavior even when she has hostile feelings. The Bible says, "Be ye angry, and sin not" (Eph. 4:26). You can help a child cope with her anger. Can you allow your child to express her feelings? If your child says, "I don't like you," when you don't let her have her way, what do you do? You will not help by saying, "Now, Paula, you know you like Mommy." When you permit your child to say how she feels, she feels free to be honest and open with you. Negative feelings which can't be expressed stay inside and breed bitterness and pity and hate. When you teach a child not to express negative feelings, she may also withhold her feelings of love.

Your child needs to see you behave as a Christian when you are experiencing different kinds of emotions. A mother was bragging that her child had never seen her cry. How does a child know when you have deep, strong emotions unless she sees you during this time? Let her see your tears of joy and your tears of sadness just as she sees you smile and hears your laughter. Your child knows when you are in control of your emotions.

Your child needs to know that she is a valuable part of the family. She feels "big" when you let her do the things around the house which she sees you doing—vacuuming, dusting, washing clothes, folding and hanging up clothes, and cooking.

If you experience the death of a loved one, your child will feel more secure if she can feel a part of the family. She feels left out and unimportant when she is sent away or put in another room away from the people. You can be frank with a child about death; she accepts what you say. She does not yet know about the finality of death. She does not worry about tomorrow. God's design for a child's development prevents the child from being burdened by adult concerns during the time when she is gaining control over her body and mind.

A child does not view life and death as adults do. She believes that a stone is alive. She judges whether an object is alive or dead according to what it is supposed to do. A pencil is alive unless it is broken, then it is dead. Even as old as seven and eight, some children think that any object that moves is alive—has a consciousness.

What Your Child Can Learn About God

The story is told about a child painting a picture who when asked to tell about it, responded, "Oh, I'm painting a picture of God."

"But nobody knows what God looks like," said her teacher.

"Well, they will when I get finished," the child replied.

To a four-year-old, who comes up with his new ideas and ways of doing things, God is most like a significant person in his life. Since a child thinks literally and not abstractly, he thinks in terms of what he can see or feel or experience through his senses. When he hears the word *God,* he thinks of him as a person (not Spirit). He has had experience with persons.

Knowing that a child is literal in his thinking, you may wonder whether you should teach him about God at this age. You know his view will be limited. What would happen on the other hand if someone so important to you as God were never mentioned? Would your child know of your own faith? We know that whatever we say about God is not easily understood. The concept of God grows with maturity, instruction, and your example of faith. A child may never mature in his concept of God unless you grow in your faith in God.

Children who live in homes with parents who do not have a growing faith in God and a commitment to follow Jesus may outgrow God in the same way they outgrow Santa Claus. They may reject God because of their childish distortions which have never been corrected. Maybe God is not real either.

A child's feelings, emotions, and attitudes about God during this year are more important than the facts he learns about God or his mental understanding of God. When you are good to your child, show love and respect for him, then he associates warm feelings and positive attitudes about the God to whom you talk and pray. Attitudes live on when facts are forgotten. If you were asked what your mother or daddy or teacher taught you about God when you were four years old, you might not remember a single thing to say. What do *you* remember? You remember that your parents were loving, that you felt loved, and that God and Jesus and the Bible and church were important to them.

When your child has distortions which can be corrected, you will be able to tell him the truth. Misconceptions are easier to change than attitudes.

Your child will talk like he understands that God is everywhere, yet he seems to want to confine God to a space. The child thinks that if God is here, then He must be under the bed. If He is here, he must be able to find Him, see Him.

If the child thinks of God in human form, he also thinks that God uses His hands to make things. He may see God as somewhat like a magician making things disappear and appear. He recognizes that God can do things which people cannot do, but his understanding of how God does it is usually distorted.

His view of heaven is somewhere that God lives and where people go when they die. If you were to ask a child where heaven is, he may point to the sky. He may say, "Clouds."

Jesus did come in human form and children can learn that He

came as a baby, He was once a child, and He grew to be a man. They know that Jesus loves them and loves other people and did things to help people. They also know that He does things they can't do, such as make sick people well. We say to them that Jesus was God's Son, but we know how difficult this is for them to understand. They do not question when we say it because they believe adults are infallible. We know that only God is infallible. If we say God is Jesus' Father (they would say Daddy), then why is Joseph the one that is with Jesus' mother? Did Jesus have two daddies? When we sing about Jesus as a baby, they think of Jesus as a baby now. They get confused. Is Jesus a baby or a man? When you say God sent Jesus, they begin to associate God with Jesus.

One child who discovered a way to distinguish the two, said, "You can't see God, but you can see Jesus." When four-year-olds who think in the here and now are told that Jesus is alive, they want to go see Him. When you say He lived a long time ago, it may mean last week to a child who has no sense of history. She hardly knows the meaning *week*.

She can learn that Jesus loved God, and God loved Jesus. She can learn many of the stories about Jesus being kind and helping others.

The Bible speaks to the importance of a child's self-image. What she thinks about herself she learns from what she sees in the mirrors of other people's faces and in the way she is treated. The child is highly sensitive to what parents think about her and her behavior.

What can a child learn about himself? When you tell him in numerous ways by words, gestures of disgust, yelling, screaming, or physical abuse, he learns that he is bad or clumsy or not enough. A child made in God's image depends on you to teach him God's love and what is right and wrong. He needs to feel good about himself and to feel that God values him and that you value him. He learns this not just from what you say but from repeated encounters with fair, respectful treatment.

How to Guide Your Child Toward God

You cannot give your child faith in God, but you can help him discover it for himself. Faith is a firsthand experience. It cannot be secondhand. You have to possess faith before you can surround your child with faith. He can sense what is real and of value to you. Your child knows if God is a vital part of your existence, that you depend on Him for guidance and comfort and submit to Him. He knows if God is personal and intimate with you or just a name He hears on Sunday at church.

Is God an important part of your everyday life experiences? If you only mention Him at meals and at bedtime, you are teaching that God is reserved just for special times of the day. The first and great commandment (Deut. 6:5-7) says that parents are to teach God's love with words—when you sit, walk, lie down, and rise up—all through the day and during all waking hours. To help your child understand God's nearness and His concern about our everyday lives, you can talk about God in the midst of your daily activities. The child learns best when he can relate what is said to what he is doing.

When Jessica's nose is pressed against the soft, fragrant petals of a rose in full bloom, she can feel the loving support of Daddy's arms around her as he says: "God made the rose for you to smell. How sweet the rose smells! God is good to give us beautiful flowers to see and smell."

As Melissa sorts the clothes or puts the silverware away, she hears you say: "Thank you for helping Mother. You put the forks and spoons and knives in their special places. I thank God for you, Melissa. I'm glad God let you be a part of our family."

When you let Aaron help make cookies to take to a friend as a Christmas gift, he is learning to share, to give what he made to another. Notice every effort to give and say: "I'm glad you wanted to give some of the cookies you made to Mrs. Sawyer. The Bible tells us to share with others."

Accept your child's uniqueness and don't compare him with anyone else. Encourage him to develop his God-given abilities.

He is just now getting a sense of humor. Laugh with him. A four-year-old in the church auditorium sat beside his mother before church worship started. His mother said he had been laughing all week about something his teacher said.

Instead of being annoyed at his humor which may not be funny to you, say: "I enjoy hearing you laugh. I am glad God made us able to laugh. I am happy when you are happy."

During this year with outbursts of anger and sometimes rage, be gentle, yet firm, with your child. If you yell, threaten your child, or lash out with physical punishment yourself, you resort to her kind of behavior and become her model for it. If you are easy to lose your temper and swift to punish, your child will think of God as out to get her. She may picture God with a big stick in His hand ready to hit her when she misbehaves. She may fear God will strike her at anytime.

An old cartoon of a father vigorously spanking his young child has this caption, "And that will teach you not to hit!" We sometimes model the very behavior we are attempting to stop. No wonder young children are confused.

If you feel secure in teaching your child, you do not need to threaten. A threat seems to say, "I can't trust you to behave."

On the other hand, when you respect your child he feels valued. As you guide him patiently and help him when he needs you, he learns to trust a loving, caring God who understands. If he feels important to his parents and his parents "do that which is right and good in the sight of the Lord" (Deut. 6:18), he learns how to be patient and gentle with others and learns to love God whom he believes loves him.

Your child will be asking questions about God. "Where is God?" "Why can't I see Him?" "Where is heaven?" You will want to answer the child simply at her level of understanding. She does not understand figurative language—language that has a second and deeper meaning—such as, "You're pulling my leg." That means teasing to an adult, but to a child it means exactly what it says. Sometimes a child wants a more simple answer than we think. Tell the child the truth which she can understand. Sometimes answer the child's question with a question, and you will know if the child has a misconception or distortion. Clarify misconceptions or distortions to help her understand better.

"Where is God?" You answer, "God is everywhere." "Why can't I see Him?" asks the child. This is a question that you might respond to with "What do you think?" so you can know where the child is in her thinking. Or you might say: "Some things we can't see. We can't see the wind, but we know it is there. We see the trees moving when the wind is blowing. We can't see God, but we can see what He made. He made the trees and the wind, and He made you and me.

"Where is heaven?" Answer, "I don't know," if that is an honest answer for you. Then add, "I do know that God made heaven, and it is more wonderful than you or I can ever think of."

Christian parents will respond somewhat differently to their children than the non-Christian parent. Even if the responses seem alike, you are guided by your loving Heavenly Father. You acknowledge that you are not your own but that you belong to God, and you live daily dependent upon His power. You have covenanted to bring your child up in the nurture and admonition of the Lord. Each day you humbly renew this commitment, knowing your own shortcomings. Your faith in God will use your limited love to guide your children toward the God who can love perfectly. God's love comes to the child through you, who know God personally and acknowledge His lordship.

When I was a child, my speech, feelings, and thinking were all those of a child (1 Cor. 13:11, GNB).

7
The Sixth Year:
Wanting to Please

Dependable, fascinating fives! What a contrast to the demanding, frustrating fours! You will think at times that she is almost too good. Mother is the center of her world, and she feels so needed. Your five-year-old likes to obey. She wants desperately to please you. She enjoys being taught and remembers to ask permission.

Physically, your child can use his body quite well and in more complex ways. He enjoys doing stunts such as somersaults and hanging upside down on a parallel bar. Now he can run, hop, and jump on two feet. He is learning to skip and jump rope. Running is his way to get to where he is going; walking is too slow. Highly active, he may not sit well for long. Even when he draws or cuts and pastes or works a puzzle, he is likely to stand rather than sit.

My! how his ability to draw, paint, color, create designs with paper and other materials has changed. His drawings are realistic. Right now he is working on shape; the right color will come later. Your child may even write his name. He is trying to write letters and numerals. A child who sees parents or other children writing wants to write, too. When you write for your child, use the kind of manuscript letters which his school uses.

If you buy clothes which your child can put on by herself, she will feel industrious. She can lace shoes and is trying to tie a bow.

Your child's behavior is much more socially acceptable at five. He can cooperate with other children his age as they build with blocks or create and transform boxes and props into a barber shop, fire station, church, or grocery store.

This is a special time when your child is searching for who he is and what kind of person he will be. He especially notices the people whose work is identified by a uniform. This is a year for seeing how it feels to be a minister, policeman, mail carrier, astronaut, mother, daddy, baby, or whatever role in life he has had the opportunity to observe. Your child will be a self-starter. He will think of work to do on his own and will do things without being told.

Mentally, your child is childish in her thinking. She does not think like adults. That is the way God made her. How she thinks mentally affects her relationships with others, what she thinks about God, Jesus, church, the Bible, things God made, and what is right and wrong.

Your five-year-old is limited and illogical. If you take two pieces of clay and roll them into balls about the same size and ask your five-year-old if each ball has the same amount, she will say yes. If you flatten one ball into a cookie shape and ask the same question, she will probably say that the flattened one has more clay. You roll the flattened one back into a ball and ask if the two balls have the same amount now, and she will say yes. When your child gets to the stage of logical thinking, she knows that if you don't add anything or take anything away, the two balls have to have the same amount even if the shape of one changes. To the young child, *seeing is believing.*

If you try to convince your child of the right answer, you only teach her that she cannot believe what she sees. You will not have taught her to think logically. She would be able to parrot a right answer to one question, but she would not know why it was the right answer except that you said so. You cannot hurry a child's thinking. She will learn to be logical with many experiences over time working with a variety of materials.

Your child has limited experience with life. He is just becoming aware of time. Time is associated with important events or activities. We go to church on *Sunday.* Cartoons come on on *Saturday.* Birthdays and Christmas are *special* occasions which mark a child's memory of time. He has little conscious memory of being two or three. So he has little understanding of history, the past or the future. He lives in the present.

He is not sure of the difference in what God made and what is man-made. He is not sure of what is dead or alive. He endows objects that move with life. Life and death have to do with ability to function according to what is intended. He is becoming aware of the finality of death but views it as a separation.

Yet unsure about cause and effect, he thinks that two things that happen near the same time, one right after the other, are related, that one causes the other. If he has just gotten angry at Daddy and has secretly wished that Daddy would go away and Daddy does go away because of divorce or separation, the child thinks he caused it.

The five-year-old is literal in his thinking. He thinks with the only experience he has. One child who was asked to name the four seasons said, "I just know three seasons: baseball, basketball, and football."

Johnny who was greeted by his aunt who had not seen him

in a year exclaimed, "Why, Johnny, you have grown another foot." Johnny looked at his feet to see if he could find it.

When Mandy's teacher asked her where her heart was, she pointed to her hip. Her teacher shook her head and said, "No, Mandy, that is not your heart."

Mandy's quick response was, "Yes, it is, too. Everytime my grandmother comes to see me, she pats me right here (Mandy pats her hip) and says, 'Bless your little heart, honey.' "

The kindergarten teacher during the Christmas season was explaining that she would bring a manger so the children would know what it looked like. She said, "And we will need some straw." Alert Diane obliged, "Oh, I'll bring the straw. I'll get it at McDonald's. We go there every Sunday night after church."

The five-year-old's language exceeds her thinking. Your child's ability to say a lot of nonsense words, cute little rhymes, the pledge of allegiance, and other songs she has heard, is most impressive. But just listen to the meaning she gets from some of the words as she substitutes her own. She may end the pledge of allegiance with something like "with liver and juice for all." Or she may have heard you end a prayer "In the name of the Father, Son, and Holy Spirit," and when she prays she closes with "In the name of the Father and the mother."

A five-year-old is self-centered. This means that your child thinks only from his point of view. He cannot put himself in the place of another and think from that point of view. In order to follow the Golden Rule, one must think from another's point of view and respond accordingly. When a person is self-centered, it is difficult for him to share for the right reasons. He is learning how to read expressions on faces and discovers that when a person receives something, he looks happy on the outside. He still thinks with what he sees, the externals. When parents do not know this characteristic of young children, they tend to misjudge the child's motives for behavior. Self-centered is not the same as selfish. To be selfish you have to have more than one view, a choice, and then choose to please yourself.

What Your Child Needs

Your child needs to feel secure in your love. He needs to know that you value him as a person. A child who is valued or recognized only for his performance feels neither loved nor safe. He feels anxious because he knows that he cannot always be the best. Today's preschoolers have many opportunities to compete in numerous contests. Your preschooler needs to be learning the gifts God gave him and improving them rather than matching his skills with others. Let your child compete only with himself, a unique person with special talents.

Many programs will vie for your child's time. Your own church may have four or more such programs. The secular world offers you ballet, swimming, aerobics, violin, beauty contests, and many others. This is the time God intended for parents to have the most influence on their children. Families need quality time together when they are relaxed. Both parents who work and those who don't will find their precious time eaten up by involvement in activities which separate rather than bring families together.

A relaxed, unhurried childhood in which a child can learn through play as he is guided by loving, caring parents who are reliant on God provides the best assurance of a mentally and spiritually healthy child and adult.

You have a great deal of power during this year when your child is so eager to please. Don't abuse your power by making your child please you. God has given individual talents to your child. Support your child's individuality. Love does not seek its own and is always proud of another's successes. Savor his gifts and help him know that God gave him the ability to use his hands to work and show kindness. Then be like Mary when she learned of her Son's potential greatness, ponder these things in your heart, and be grateful unto God, not flaunting them before your friends.

Your child needs your encouragement in her search for self. Enjoy her questions. Allow her to explain, explore, manipulate objects, and test her surroundings. Your child is capable of marvelous inventions. Notice how she goes about "cooking," "caring for the baby," and what she paints, draws, and constructs with blocks or other materials. Watch her transform "beautiful junk" into castles, fortresses, hospitals, tunnels, skyscrapers. In her struggle to discover herself and her surroundings, enjoy her fantasy of flying over buildings, diving to the depth of the ocean, landing on the moon, and becoming the animals and people she has experienced.

Your child feels safe and secure when your discipline (teaching) is consistent, when she knows what to expect and knows that you will not embarrass or be rude to her. She learns that you trust her to do what is right, and she wants to please you.

Your child needs your understanding that he is limited and illogical, that he makes judgments on how things appear to him. If you pour one child some juice in a short, fat glass and another child the same amount of juice in a tall, skinny glass, the child will notice the level of the juice. The glass in which the juice appears to be higher to your child will have more juice. He will think that you are unfair to give him the short glass. You will understand his thinking and try to use glasses of the same size and shape.

Your child needs your understanding that she puts the only meaning she has into words and her meaning may not be the meaning you had intended. This frequently happens with biblical material with which the child has had little or no experience.

As a child was looking at the picture of the baby Jesus in the manger, he said, "There's Wayne." His mother asked, "What makes you think that is Wayne?"

"Well, because we sing 'Awayne in a manger,' " he replied.

Another misconception is illustrated by the story which is told about the child who drew a picture of an airplane with a pilot and three passengers: a man, a woman, and a baby. When asked to tell about her picture the child said, "Oh, that's Pon-ti-us, the pilot, and that's Mary and Joseph and the baby on their flight to Egypt."

She needs you to understand that she is self-centered. When you put adult intent into your child's behavior you may misconstrue it for moral badness. If you see from your child's point of view, you will understand that she does not know how her actions affect others.

A five-year-old was singing "Jesus Loves Me" with her mother. She said, "You sing, 'Jesus loves *you*' and I'll sing 'Jesus love *me.*' " From her point of view her mother was *you* and that's what she should sing.

Your child needs you to understand that he cannot remember several things at the same time. If you ask your child not to run in the house, he thinks you have made a request, not a rule. So, when he runs in the house tomorrow, you will know that he is not deliberately disobeying. You will need to state a rule many times before he remembers the conditions: time, place, and circumstance. He finds it difficult to remember the three things at one time. You let him run in one room of the house on a rainy day if company is not using the family room.

Your child needs for you to understand that sharing is difficult. When you are an example or model of sharing, your child learns to share. Julie, who had strung beads while her mother made Easter baskets to give away, gave her string of beads to a favored guest one evening. Julie had truly shared, given something which she had made to someone else.

What Your Child Can Learn About God

Try to recall your earliest remembrance of what God looked like? Was He an old man with a long beard who could do things you could not do? Your child thinks of God as having human form and along with that she places her notions about what God is like drawn from her experiences with you and other important people in her world. Hopefully, among these are her teachers at church and her grandparents. Your relationship to your child, the way you treat her, and what you say about God fashions in her mind her first thoughts about Him.

A child who had just watched an educational television program attempting to teach the difference between real and imaginary said to her mother, "God is imaginary."

Mother responded, "You think God is imaginary because you can't see him, but God is real. You can see the things God planned for us to have. You can see the flowers, animals, fish, moon, stars, and grass which God gives to us."

Two preschoolers making noise in a hallway were approached by the minister of education who showed them to their room. Later, when the two boys were walking with their parents by the minister of education's office, they saw him seated in a chair and announced, "There's God."

One child thought that the dog which he had seen at the back of the parsonage which was adjacent to the church parking lot was Jesus' dog. He associates *church* with God and Jesus.

If you use the words *God's house,* he expects to find Him there. If you say God lives in heaven, the child may feel confused. Because he is literal, the word *church* seems more appropriate than God's house.

Your child's view of *church* is usually limited to the externals on which she focuses—the pews from which her legs dangle, the colored windows, the big cross on the church billboard, the pulpit, the baptistry (she finds this most intriguing). A child is getting foundations for the concept of church as a fellowship as she has satisfying experiences with teachers and children at church where she sings songs, looks at pictures, and hears Bible stories and verses which relate to her everyday life.

A child can understand *offering* better than God's money or Jesus' money because he never sees God or Jesus with the money. He can learn about specific things his offerings buy: hymnals, Bibles, furniture, lights, heat, and water.

Sitting for an hour in a worship service may be as trying for your five-year-old as it would be for you to stand for an entire service. Hopefully, if your child attends church rather than the extended session of Sunday School which occurs during the worship service, the service has some special elements with which the child can relate, such as a song he knows, some Bible verses or a Bible story he understands, or a special time with the pastor.

Worship is an abstract term. If you ask your child "Why do we go to church?" he may not give the reasons you had hoped that would sound more spiritual. He might say, "To drink juice, paint pictures, play with Michael, sing songs, hear a Bible story, read the Bible." What he says is what he *thinks*. He is telling you what he notices that is important to him. You can teach him a right answer such as "We go to church to worship God," but you may not have changed his thinking. He needs to hear you say what worship is in specific terms. We worship God when we tell him we love Him, when we sing about His love, when we thank Him, when we read from the Bible how to behave.

If your main concern during a worship service is to keep your child quiet and still, he may come to think of worship as a physical posture more than communicating with God.

When Can Your Child Believe?

When can your child believe in Jesus' sacrificial death and turn in repentance toward God through faith in Christ Jesus? When is your child accountable to God rather than you for his choices? This subject is a sensitive one deserving our careful and prayerful attention. What parent does not want his child to experience salvation, wholeness through Christ, abundant life here, and eternal life with God! We want our children to have a genuine encounter with God through Christ, not a premature external experience of walking the aisle, shaking a pastor's hand, saying "I'm sorry" for my sins (whatever that is to the child), and saying "I want to be baptized; I want to join the church." We do not want cheap grace for our children.

Dietrich Bonhoeffer in his book *The Cost of Discipleship* speaks of cheap grace as forgiveness without repentance, baptism without submitting to church discipline (obedient to its teachings), and communion without confession of sins. This is a grace without discipleship and without Jesus Christ living within.

Some parents are overly zealous in wanting their child to have assurance of heaven that they rush the child toward a decision for Christ. Other adults believe that salvation is a commitment to follow Christ, to entrust their lives to His guidance, and to live for Him assured of His living presence within them. *Salvation is life's most important decision and requires maturity.*

You are the child's authority to whom he is accountable until he reaches the age when he is accountable to God for his actions, his choices. You teach him what is right and wrong by what you stop and what you allow. He trusts that you know what is right. You are infallible to him. You help to develop in him a conscience. Your child does not judge rightness and wrongness on the basis of what the Bible says but on what you say. His moral judgments are based on what he sees. To be accountable a person must know what is right and wrong in the sight of God, not just in the sight of his parents. Let us not confuse conscience which is learned with the work of the Holy Spirit.

Repentance is a vital part of salvation. A child has to know what sin is before he can ask forgiveness and turn from his sin.

Recently, an evangelist was appealing to young children to walk the aisle and get saved. "Take your mother by the hand and come on down to the altar and the preacher will tell you how to be saved." Remember young children want to please, they trust adults to tell them what is right, they want to do what is right. A seven-year-old took her mother's hand and said, "Come on, Mother, let's go." The mother sat down with the child quietly and said, "Have you ever sinned against God?"

The child answered, "Oh, no, I love God, I would never do that."

When you or a pastor asks your child questions all of which can be answered *yes,* your child may just be cooperating with what she thinks you want her to do. If you ask her if she loves Jesus, if she wants to follow Jesus, if she wants to give her heart to Jesus, she will say *yes.* She may just be imitating what she has heard and seen other children and adults do.

What five-year-old doesn't love Jesus if her parents have

taught her to by word and example? A child's statement that she loves Jesus is not to be mistaken for salvation.

Can your child accept the responsibility for his actions, or are you still responsible for them? What choices do you allow your child to make? Can he decide whether or not he goes to church? to school? Can he decide if he will drive the car, get married, buy his own clothes, spend the night away from home, join the army, smoke a cigarette? Why is it that we think a child is ready to make life's highest choice when we do not hold him accountable for relatively simple decisions?

How Can You Guide Your Child Toward God?

As you view your child's relationship toward God and Jesus, consider these things: (1) your child's limited experience and literal thinking which is in keeping with God's design for the early years, (2) your child's need to please to get your approval or recognition, (3) Jesus' example with little children, (4) what Jesus said about their spiritual status ("of such is the kingdom of heaven"), (5) when Jesus was considered accountable (at or about the age of twelve), (6) when Jesus was baptized (at or about age thirty), (7) the absence of examples of young children being baptized recorded in Scripture, and (8) Jesus' admonition about our treatment of little children: "Take heed that ye despise not one of these little ones; for I say unto you, That in heaven their angels do always behold the face of my Father which is in heaven" (Matt. 18:10).

What a tragedy when little children are allowed to go through the externals of confessing Christ and being baptized with water thinking that they have done what they are supposed to do—only to discover as an adult that they have never had a valid, personal experience with Christ and have been living a borrowed religion or a secondhand faith!

Accept your own accountability for your child during this time when he is responsible to you. Love God with all your being. Love your spouse and show it in tangible ways. Love your child as a gift of God made in the image of God. Treat your child with the same respect that you treat your friends. Treat your child as you would like to be treated. Spend time with your family doing things the family enjoys. Childhood passes swiftly, and the grand opportunities to train up your child in the way he should go (see Prov. 22:6) are gone forever.

Share with your child your love for the Bible and your need to know what it says. Use its stories and truths throughout the day and night when your child can relate it to the ongoing activity. Many times you will be able to say, "God planned . . . ." "God planned for us to have milk to drink. Milk comes from cows." "God planned for us to have eggs. Eggs come from chickens." Give your child opportunities for many firsthand experiences with the sources of the food you eat, the clothes you wear, the house you live in, to get him in touch with God as Creator.

At five, she is beginning to question "how things are made." If a baby comes from a hospital, she thinks it is made there and you buy the baby there like you do food from the store. She wonders how God made the baby when she knows its source: the hospital.

The child thinks magically. A magician can make a rabbit appear. He thinks that the magician made the rabbit. He accepts what he sees. At age five, instead of saying, "God made the baby" which may create misconceptions of how God made the baby, you may want to say, "God planned for a baby to have a mother and a daddy."

Many opportunities will arise for you to show reverence and awe for the wonders of God. When Mother and Daddy spend

a family time together at the park, Jonathan and his younger
sister Rachel see the mother and daddy ducks and their babies.
This is a special time for each child to feel loved. Mother stoops
down and puts her hand on Jonathan's waist as they look at the
white ducks waddling all around them. Daddy squats and puts
his hand around in front of Rachel touching her gently and
protecting her from the water in front of them. "Jonathan, the
ducks are curious. They are coming to see who we are," says
Mother. "Rachel sees the fuzzy little ducklings swimming in the
water. I am glad God made the ducks and their babies for
Jonathan and Rachel to see," says Daddy.

A child is just beginning to understand the natural world
which God made. In order to understand the supernatural
(miracles), a child must understand what is natural.

The child has a limited view of cause and effect. He looks at
a tree and takes its presence for granted. A child has to learn
through many firsthand experiences with seed and animals and
people to discover the majesty of God's creations in his natural
world.

When you tell about Jesus helping to make the blind man see
or the sick man well, he may not consider that supernatural.
Doctors make sick people well, too. Every time you tell him
stories about how Jesus helped people which are miracles from
your point of view, tell your child that Jesus did this because He
loved the man.

Parables are symbolic. The child can learn the story of "The
Lost Sheep" but to him it is about a sheep, not about a lost
person. Many songs and hymns are symbolic, such as "This
Little Light of Mine" and "Are You Washed in the Blood?"

Bible stories for preschoolers need to be selected carefully so
that the child learns that the Bible is about something she can
understand, and it has to do with living. Some Bible stories are

beyond the child's comprehension. "David and Goliath" may be a favorite story, but what can the child learn from it that affects his daily living? He may think that it is all right to kill. The hero of the story killed someone. Even adults have difficulty coming to grips with the commandment "Thou shalt not kill" (Ex. 20:13) and if and when it is all right to kill. Little children cannot understand why the Bible says not to kill in one place and lauds a hero who has killed in another.

In like manner, what can a child learn from "Daniel in the Lion's Den?" She may learn that she can play with dangerous animals, and God will protect her.

Bible content should be at the child's level of understanding. We learn what we can understand and what we need to know.

Better that a child hear Bible truths repeatedly when they relate to what he is doing and can be understood than to memorize verses that he doesn't understand because "someday he will need them."

Don't expect of your child what you are not willing to do yourself. What Bible verses have you memorized lately that you did not understand for the reason that you would need them later on?

Watch that you don't teach too much too soon! The child needs to understand and apply the information with love and joy.

"Dear friends, let us practice loving each other, for love comes from God and those who are loving and kind show that they are the children of God" (1 John 4:7, TLB).

I pray that your love will keep on growing more and more, together with true knowledge and perfect judgment, . . . Your lives will be filled with the truly good qualities which only Jesus Christ can produce, for the glory and praise of God (Phil. 1:9,11, GNB).

8
Your Most Important Job

Where are you in your spiritual journey? As Christians, we are admonished to grow toward Christian maturity—becoming increasingly more Christlike. Your most important job is to grow in your Christian faith, share your faith with others, and help your child discover his faith. You do this by your actions, helping your child experience God's love.

You are totally dependent on God (your authority) for your total needs (physical, mental, social, emotional, moral, spiritual), even to each breath of life. Your dependence upon God is not a crutch or an attempt to neglect responsibility but a source of strength and wisdom and guidance. God and you are enough to help you grow in oneness with God and to help your family grow in love.

As you share your faith with your child, you discover that the best way to understand what you believe is to put it into words your child can understand. You will have opportunities during the routines of living to apply your faith to life in both planned and unplanned moments. Be alert to opportunities for spontaneous sharing. Also, create opportunities by planning to share experiences at mealtime, before naps and bedtime, and other family times.

What Is Christian Faith?

Christian faith is your complete trust and dependency in the person Jesus Christ, God's Son, in order to make life meaningful and worthwhile. I have used the following steps by ages to help you see how faith may grow toward maturity through age periods. Just as a child's physical, mental, social, and moral development grows through stages or steps at or about certain ages, so does his spiritual development grow. A person's spiritual journey may sometimes be slow and sometimes fast, sometimes forward and at other times backward. However, the steps on the journey seem to follow the same pattern as the ages and stages of life—from birth until mature adult or from the spiritual new birth until spiritual maturity.

Step 1—Age of Infancy

In infancy spiritual foundations are laid. The spiritual qualities of trust, hope, and love emerge or distrust, doubt, despair, and hate take root. You are the one to determine whether the positive or negative qualities occur. The tender, loving care and quiet confidence of parents can best bestow these qualities during the first few years of life. If not developed during these years, the spiritual qualities of trust, faith, hope, and love become increasingly more difficult to nurture and more difficult to acquire.

As your child learns to trust you for what he cannot do for himself, you can trust God to lovingly care for your needs. God wants you to do for yourself what you can do. He ably equips you to cope with your earthly life. God is with you and within you. His spirit encourages and assures you of His love and peace.

God offers to each of us the opportunity to experience new life—eternal life. With this new life comes meaning, power, and peace for this earthly part of our journey. The Bible tells us how this quality of life here and forever after is possible. This new life is a gift of God (Rom. 6:23). The gift cannot be earned. It is yours when you accept it (Eph. 2:8-9).

God is the source of love—"God is love" (1 John 4:8). God is a personal being wanting to love us, talk with us, and meet our needs. God loved us so much that He was willing to conform to all His laws of human growth and development and be born of woman as you and I. He was born a baby dependent upon His earthly parents and followed the same patterns of growth we follow. He knew what it was like to be a child, a young person, and an adult. Truly He was willing to be tempted in all points as we are. How humbling!

"Greater love hath no man than this, that a man lay down his life for his friends" (John 15:13). Truly He laid down His life through living it, only to find it again. From the moment of conception He became like we are, born to endure the same life struggles and yet to be triumphant in life and in death. He lived, He died, He lives. You can follow the same pattern.

One of my favorite Bible passages is: "Let us love one another, because love comes from God. Whoever loves is a child of God and knows God" (1 John 4:7, GNB). Each of us falls short of God's standard and will fall short all of our lives. We are helpless before God. We are dependent upon Him for life everlasting. Before Jesus, animals were laid on the altar to atone for sins. Jesus atoned for our sins. Through a personal relationship with Jesus, He offers us life eternal.

Jesus said, "I am the way, the truth, and the life; no one goes to the Father except by me" (John 14:6, GNB). When we accept God's gift and what Christ has done in our behalf, His way becomes our way, His truth becomes our truth, and His life our life. We begin a new life (see 2 Cor. 5:17).

To know Christ is to know God. Have you experienced the spiritual birth of which Jesus speaks in John 3:1-18? A teacher of Israel, a man of authority among the Jews named Nicodemus, went to see Jesus at night. He addressed Jesus as Rabbi or Teacher come from God.

Jesus solemnly told Nicodemus that he could not experience the kingdom of God unless he was born from above. Nicodemus was confused by this talk of a rebirth. How could he enter his mother's womb again?

Jesus mentioned his physical birth, being born of water, and then he talked about his spiritual birth. Through physical birth you enter an earthly life; through the birth of the Spirit you enter the kingdom of God.

Being born of the Spirit is of God. Just as God made the wind to blow and you breathe it, hear it, and see it, but you do not know where it comes from nor where it goes, so is the birth of the Spirit. We feel it, we experience it, but we cannot see its source.

Jesus told Nicodemus that the Son of man (Himself) had come from heaven to earth. Nicodemus listened as Jesus explained how He would be lifted up (die on a cross) as Moses lifted up the serpent on the pole in the desert so that those who looked to it in faith would be healed. Those who trust in Jesus, who allowed Himself to be lifted up, can be healed also. Those who look to Him in faith are assured that they will not perish but will have everlasting life—abundant life here and forever.

Step 2—Age of Childhood

The next step usually occurs between ages three through eleven. Most all people in their spiritual journey pass through this period. Children at this age are self-centered. This is not the same as selfish. They have a limited view, their own. A person has to be able to think from another's point of view before he can have two views. For a child to be selfish, he must have more than one person's view and still choose his own. Adults in this spiritual age are self-centered. Self-centered adults are selfish because they have the mental capacity to put themselves in the place of another but do not yet do so.

During this stage the child who is not yet logical tries to make sense out of a world of symbolism and abstractions. So much of the language used to describe spiritual things which are abstract is largely symbolic. The cross, baptism, bread and cup (fruit of the vine) used in the Lord's Supper, although they are tangible, are symbols of much deeper meanings. The cross is a recognizable object, but it symbolizes God's sacrifice of love, giving Himself to us all that through Him we might have life. Baptism is a symbol of death to the old person and resurrection to a newness of life in Christ. The bread and juice used in the Lord's Supper represent His sacrifice, and we eat and drink to remember what He did and to look forward to the day of His appearing. *Grace, salvation, redemption, mercy, love, justification, and santification* are all difficult terms to explain to a child who is limited and illogical in his thinking—even when he has materials in his hands with which to think. Some adults find these terms difficult.

The child is literal minded, that is, he has mental pictures of things which are otherwise abstract. He thinks of God as a person most like a parent or another important adult in his life.

The literal-minded child hears many words to which he must give his own meaning. The word *heart* is used frequently. The child first learns that the heart is the part of the body near the center of the rib cage. Christians use the word *heart* to have a deeper meaning. The young child thinks only of a part of the body. A four-year-old who had seen a heart transplant on television was upset when the pastor appealed to the congregation to "give your hearts to Jesus." Her mental picture of giving your heart was of a person cutting her chest open, removing her heart, and handing it to Jesus. She left the service saying, "I don't want to give my heart to Jesus."

Are you self-centered? Concerned about pleasing yourself without considering others' needs? Do symbols of the faith have a deep spiritual meaning for you, or do you think any deeper than the tangible symbol? If a child partakes of the Lord's Supper, he may think only of eating bread and drinking juice. To those who are mature in the faith, the symbols represent a deeper spiritual meaning. As the Lord's Supper is being administered, the mature Christian will think of the death of Christ with His broken body (bread) and His spilled blood (the fruit of the vine) given in a sacrificial act of love. He thanks God for Christ's coming to earth in the form of flesh and blood and living a life for us to follow. As you partake, do you look with hope to Christ's coming again? He said, "Do this in remembrance of me whenever you drink it" (1 Cor. 11:25, TLB).

The child is both self-centered (although he is growing away from it) and literal minded. He thinks that the rule is: "Do unto others what they do unto you." The child who is told by parents, "If he hits, you hit him back" is the child who is always hitting back first.

Also in this spiritual age the child, youth, or adult relies on the authority of another. He depends on others to tell him what to do and what to think.

Step 3—Age of Youth

This stage is typical for adolescents and adults. During adolescence the peer group has a strong influence in the physical and spiritual journey. At this stage the group and its values have a powerful influence upon the person. People at this stage are attracted by winsome and dynamic preachers. They may be more swayed by the drama than by the message. They may enjoy and listen to such people and having done so have fulfilled their responsibility to worship. They may have listened and applauded the words, but their lives may not have changed significantly.

A person may have ambition to become like the man but may not have ambition to become like Christ. In this age there is a strong dependence on others who have the answers. They trust others who *know* for them. These persons doubt their own competence in seeking answers from the Bible with the help of God's Spirit. They may believe that spiritual beliefs can be tied up in a neat little bundle and a person's denomination has all the right answers. They may believe that when one joins, he has the answers, too. Yet the Bible teaches that each person is accountable for his own relationship and walk with God.

Step 4—Young Adult Age

In this age the person is on his own. A person goes out into the world to make his mark. He has a love relationship with his parents, but she is no longer dependent on them economically, emotionally, or spiritually. In the spiritual journey these persons take life seriously. They are responsible for their attitudes, what they believe, and how they live. They often go through a period of painful self-examination. *Do I believe what I believe because my parents believe it, my teachers taught this, or because I believe it? I'm no longer comfortable; in fact, I am miserable accepting someone else's faith.* This can be a traumatic experience for those who for the first time discover they have been living a borrowed religion, a secondhand faith. They have come to question: *Who am I? Why am I here? Why do I believe what I believe? What am I to do with my life? What belief in my head and on my tongue do I reveal in my behavior? What does the Bible really teach?*

This type of maturity comes later for some and is often brought on by a traumatic event which causes a rupture in life's smooth regularity. A crisis, such as death, divorce, terminal or irreversible disease, children leaving home, loss of job, or loss by natural disaster, can cause one to reflect on the purpose of life. This person begins to feel a deep spiritual yearning to make sense out of all of life. He comes to grip with a gnawing desire to know the truth. He reflects on his life, his childhood and youth, where he has been, and where he is going. *Is there more to life than this? What am I missing out on?*

One comes to the conclusion that surely life is more than this flat, sterile existence. Life *is more.* Life is to be savored. Every fleeting moment of it is sacred, a precious commodity. Every breath is a miracle. *I am beginning to experience life at its fullest*—the abundant life referred to in John 10:10. *I want the same abundant life for everyone else.* Thus, this person is propelled into the next higher age.

Step 5—Middle Adult Age

Who among us reaches this spiritual age? The person in this age can see the finer, smaller things which evade the naked eye, and at the same time he can see the vastness of an infinite universe. He is in touch with heaven and with earth. He can find meaning for the present from the past. A person gains a perspective of the wholeness of life—the meaning of each age. And he grasps the significance of each step of his journey which helps him live the present to the fullest and approach the future with assurance and ambition to become all God made him able to become. He relishes being who he is and where he is on his journey. He looks back, not in despair, but with a desire to learn from the past so he can look forward with hope. He lives each day as his last because he knows it is the only day for which he can be sure. Given a choice of what age he would like to be, he shows no desire to return to the past. He lives fully in today and looks forward to tomorrow.

He sees the world's needs, and he longs to be a part of meeting these needs. On the one hand this person wants to give all of himself to the cause of Christ. He wants to help everyone know about God's love, the love he showed in coming to earth in the form of a baby, his life of ministry to human and spiritual needs, his willingness to suffer and die to give hope to all people, his resurrection which gives us faith in our own immortality and our eternal destiny with God. On the other hand, he feels constrained to preserve his own way of life and that of the people he loves. He feels strongly about his mission for Christ but may be unwilling to sacrifice greatly to achieve the cause.

Step 6—Older Adult Age

In this age, the final step, few people doubtless enter. The people at this spiritual age will risk, and if need be, give up life to realize a dream. Like Jesus, they may die at the hands of the ones they are trying to save. Some are willing to die for a cause but may not have to. Others are willing to die, fully conscious that death is imminent. Those in this stage may appear more simple. They have learned the discipline of simplicity. When you hear a great pianist playing a work of Bach, you may think, "How simple and clear that sounds, and how easy it is for her to play." Just the opposite is true. The disciplined pianist makes it sound that way.

Spiritual life at this level seems more simple just as the earthly life of Jesus seemed—but how profound it was. Fully human—fully divine, He loved life, but He could let it go. He loved all people. He was no respecter of persons. He loves you at any age on your journey. People in this age of faith are open and loving to all people, knowing that they are made in the image of God and that God came to earth through Jesus and died for each of them that each might have life.

How logical and reasonable that the last age of the spiritual journey ends at the level which Jesus so nobly demonstrated! Jesus accepted people in all ages of their journey. We are to love people not because of who they are but because they are made in the image of God and because God loved us when we were yet unlovely. We can love each person whether he or she is the age of a child, youth, or adult physically or spiritually. Each of us is on a journey, and we travel according to our age, our mental abilities, our attitudes, and our motivation to become all God planned for us to become.

Jesus was willing to give up His life for His cause. He came with the purpose of revealing God's love, of setting people free from bondage, of giving hope in this life and for the life to come. He followed His "dream." He lived out His destiny. He relinquished His family ties. Remember the occasion when His mother and brothers came and, when told of their presence, He inquired, "Who is my mother and my brother?" (see Mark 3:33). His destiny was one of pain and grief, yet through His death He brought life to all those who believed in Him. Those persons who arrive at this age, for which they probably never seek, will also find that when they give up life for their cause, they, too, will suffer pain and grief. But such a person loses life only to find it again.

Each person should have a sense of destiny—a belief that *I am come to the Kingdom for just such a time as this.* You have been born to live out your destiny. You have special gifts. There is no one else in the whole world (never has been, nor is, nor ever shall be) just like you. Savor your uniqueness. Cultivate your gifts. There are some people whose lives you can touch in ways no other person can. You are the only *you* God made. *Be all that you can be.* You are made in the image of God. God loves you. You are a "designer's original." God has a purpose for your life. You are valuable and worthwhile.

TV commercials bid you to become all that you can be, and they designate the place. In one commercial it's "in the army." From both the secular and spiritual vocations come the challenge, "Be all that you can be." Many of these, however, lack the knowledge of the source of life and love. How can you be all that you can be without knowing the Source of dynamic life and love? God is our Creator, Maker, Designer. "It is he that hath made us, and not we ourselves" (Ps. 100:3).

And it is He who made you able to become all that you can become. Can you say to yourself these words? I am responsible, able, and capable, but I cannot pull my own strings. I depend upon God for the whole of me—my life, my breath, my mind, my body, my spirit. His power within this body which He fashioned is my source of life and love. I pray to become an instrument in His hands living life at its fullest because it is He and not I who lives within. I am steadfastly conforming to Jesus' example in living (see Matt. 10:38). To him be the glory of any loving act or deed which comes from me.

May this be your prayer

"Now to Him who is able to do exceeding abundantly beyond all that we ask or think, according to the power that works within us, to Him be the glory in the church and in Christ Jesus to all generations forever and ever" (Eph. 3:20-21, NASB).

Where Are You on Your Spiritual Journey?

"God has chosen you from the beginning" (2 Thess. 2:13, NASB).

"Rejoice, be made complete, be comforted, be like-minded, live in peace; and the God of love [Who is the Source] and peace shall be with you" (2 Cor. 13:11, NASB).

Both religious and nonreligious people have faith, but in the Christian faith a person's trust is in God through Christ. This makes life worthwhile. Life takes on new meaning. A growing love relationship begins and continues.

INFANCY

_____ Do you trust God as your young child (birth through two) trusts you as the source of nourishment and love in your life?

CHILDHOOD AGE

(Typically a child three through eleven, but some adults are also in this stage.)

_____ Are you self-centered? Still thinking from your own point of view without putting yourself in another person's place to think what he needs or wants?

_____ Are you literal in your thinking? That is, do you have a concrete or mental image of God as a person as opposed to a spirit which has no mental image. Do the symbols of the cross, baptism, bread, and cup have only surface meaning, not the deeper spiritual meanings and messages for your life?

_____ Is seeing believing? A child sees something that is illogical to an adult but accepts it because he sees it. Do you base your judgments on externals without considering another person's motives?

_____ Do you obey just to avoid punishment?

_____ Do you follow the rules only when an authority figure is in sight? (Do you obey the speed limit only when you know a highway patrol is in sight or nearby?)

_____ Does your ability to talk about spiritual truths exceed your knowledge of their real meaning? Do you *talk* more Bible truths than you live? Words are easy to say. Love, kindness, patience, and helpfulness are difficult to practice.

_____ Do you believe in retribution, "an eye for an eye"? (If you get hit, you hit the person who hits you. "He hit me first" makes it all right for you to hit back.)

YOUTH AGE

_____ Do you let others do your spiritual thinking for you? Do you depend on earthly teachers to be the authority over you as opposed to seeking God's will and way for your life through studying the Bible and listening to His Spirit.

_____ Are you a conformist? That is, are you more concerned about what others think than what you think about God's will and way?

_____ Do you lack a sense of your identity, uniqueness, ministry, and destiny?

YOUNG ADULT AGE

_____ Do you know what you believe? Who you are? Why you are here? What you are to do with your life?

MIDDLE ADULT AGE

_____ Do you see all of life—yours and others of the world's population—through God's eyes? Do you have a world vision and the longing to meet the needs you see?

_____ Can you view life as a whole and fit the parts into the picture?

_____ Do you see each person as made in the image of God, one for whom Christ lived and died?

OLDER ADULT AGE

_____ Do you accept and love all people no matter where they are in their spiritual journey?

_____ Are you willing to live fully for the cause of Christ and if need be to die for it?

"May our Lord Jesus Christ himself and God our Father, who has loved us and given us everlasting comfort and hope which we don't deserve, comfort your hearts with all comfort, and help you in every good thing you say and do" (2 Thess. 2:16, TLB).

Understanding Yourself

Do you get upset with your child for no good reason? Do you make unreasonable demands of your child and yourself? Do you wish you understood your child better? Yourself better?

How important it is to understand yourself! Understanding yourself and your own behavior is the point of beginning for changing what you find inappropriate. Your behavior not only determines your successes and happiness, but greatly determines your child's development as a person made in the image of God. Your behavior gives your child her most lasting impressions of the world, who she is, who you are, and what God is like.

Your expressions and gestures, smiles and frowns, laughter and reprimands, approval and disapproval, and your satisfaction and displeasure combine to shape the personality of your child. Your child is sensitive to your emotions even when he cannot understand your words. The way you behave toward your child determines his behavior. He seems to take on your values, your moods, your responses to life, your prejudices, and your assurance or your frustration. Take a moment to think about yourself and your child.

Your child is unique, one of a kind, with her own individual gifts and bent. You are also unique. No two parents are alike. No two children are alike. Each child in a family has a different environment. Each parent has a different parenting style. Though parents may relate differently to a child, each parent can choose to follow the truth, "A wise teacher makes learning a joy" (Prov. 15:2, TLB). Each can teach the child that she is valuable and worthwhile, able and capable, and supply her with the materials and emotional encouragement for learning and developing into the person God made her able to be.

As you guide your child, you can be fully aware that God is ever near, around you and within you, quickening you with knowledge and faith to meet life's every challenge. So, rely on God, have faith in His promises, know yourself and keep on becoming. Know your child and tune in to your child's needs, interests, and readiness to learn God's love and ways.

If you love God with all your being and you know that God made you in his image, then you can feel valuable and worthwhile. God loves you. God made you. You are valuable and worthwhile. You can love yourself, respect yourself as among God's highest creation. When you love and respect yourself, you are best able to help your child know that he, too, is valuable and worthwhile. Your relationship to your child is one of respect. Your child-rearing style is democratic.

If you feel that you are valuable and worthwhile, but your child is not, then you will likely be a disrespectful parent. You will think "Big I" and "Little you." Your child-rearing practice is largely authoritarian.

If you think your child is not valuable and worthwhile and you are not, then you have no respect for yourself or your child. You are abusive, neglectful, and disrespectful. You go to extremes. Your parenting style is inconsistent.

If you feel that you are not valuable and worthwhile, but your child is, then you are indulgent. You do not deserve anything; your child deserves all of you and everything else. You are indulgent, giving in to your child's whims and unreasonable demands. You let your child behave in ways that are annoying, hurtful, and destructive without stopping these behaviors that intrude on the rights of others. Your child-rearing style is overly permissive.

The second great commandment, "Love your neighbor as you love yourself" (Mark 12:31, GNB) and the Golden Rule, "Therefore all things whatsoever ye would that men should do to you, do ye even so to them" (Matt. 7:12) place high worth and value on each person. These are guiding principles for human relationships under God. Deuteronomy 6:5-7, the first and great commandment, and verse 18 challenge us to love with all our being and teach God's love and ways by our words and example throughout the normal everyday occurrences of life. Love is the key to guiding your child to God. So, love God, love yourself, and love your child. "Love is patient and kind; it is not jealous or conceited or proud; love is not ill-mannered or selfish or irritable; love does not keep a record of wrongs; love is not happy with evil, but is happy with the truth. Love never gives up; and its faith, hope, and patience never fail" (1 Cor. 13:4-7, GNB).

Guiding your child toward God is a rewarding accomplishment when you commit your life and your child "unto him that is able to do exceeding abundantly above all that we ask or think, according to the power that worketh in us" (Eph. 3:20).

Appendix:
Read-to-Me Bible

The Read-to-Me Edition of the Bible published by Holman is designed especially for use with young children. It includes appropriate Bible stories, pictures, a list of appropriate Bible verses and thoughts, and helps on guiding the child's spiritual development. The following stories are included.

God Made Night and Day
God Made Flowers, Grass, and
   Trees
God Made People
Adam Names the Animals
Noah and the Animals
Rachel and the Sheep
Joseph's Coat
Miriam Watches Her Family
Ruth Finds Grain for Food
Hannah Talks with God
Samuel at Church
David Cares for the Sheep
David and Jonathan
Elisha's Friends
King Josiah Reads the Bible
Solomon Builds a Church

God Made the Birds
Daniel Chooses Good Food
Mary's Good News
Jesus Was Born
Shepherds Visit Jesus
Wise Men Bringing Gifts
Baby Jesus at Church
A Trip for Jesus
Boy Jesus at Church
Jesus Chooses Helpers
Jesus Reads from the Bible
Jesus and the Blind Man
The Kind Man
Four Friends Who Helped
Jesus and the Woman with the
   Crooked Back
The Man Who Said Thank You

Jesus Sees Zacchaeus
Jesus Talks with the Woman at
   the Well
Jesus and the Children
A Boy Shares His Lunch
Jesus Visits Mary and Martha
Children Sang for Jesus

A Happy Day (Easter)
Dorcas Helped People
Paul and Barnabas Bringing
   Good News
Timothy and His Mother
Lydia Hears About Jesus
Paul, Aquila, and Priscilla